D0081884

The population history of
Britain and Ireland
1500–1750

New Studies in Economic and Social History

Edited for the Economic History Society by
Michael Sanderson
University of East Anglia, Norwich

This series, specially commissioned by the Economic History Society, provides a guide to the current interpretations of the key themes of economic and social history in which advances have recently been made or in which there has been significant debate.

In recent times economic and social history has been one of the most flourishing areas of historical study. This has mirrored the increasing relevance of the economic and social sciences both in a student's choice of career and in forming a society at large more aware of the importance of these issues in their everyday lives. Moreover specialist interests in business, agricultural and welfare history, for example, have themselves burgeoned and there has been an increased interest in the economic development of the wider world. Stimulating as these scholarly developments have been for the specialist, the rapid advance of the subject and the quantity of new publications make it difficult for the reader to gain an overview of particular topics, let alone the whole field.

New Studies in Economic and Social History is intended for students and their teachers. It is designed to introduce them to fresh topics and to enable them to keep abreast of recent writing and debates. All the books in the series are written by a recognised authority in the subject, and the arguments and issues are set out in a critical but unpartisan fashion. The aim of the series is to survey the current state of scholarship, rather than to provide a set of prepackaged conclusions.

The series has been edited since its inception in 1968 by Professors M. W. Flinn, T. C. Smout and L. A. Clarkson, and is currently edited by Dr Michael Sanderson. From 1968 it was published by Macmillan as *Studies in Economic History*, and after 1974 as *Studies in Economic and Social History*. From 1995 *New Studies in Economic and Social History* is being published on behalf of the Economic History Society by Cambridge University Press. This new series includes some of the titles previously published by Macmillan as well as new titles, and reflects the ongoing development throughout the world of this rich seam of history.

For a full list of titles in print, please see the end of the book.

The population history of Britain and Ireland 1500–1750

Prepared for the Economic History Society by

R. A. Houston
University of St Andrews

Published by the Press Syndicate of the University of Cambridge
The Pitt Building, Trumpington Street, Cambridge CB2 1RP
40 West 20th Street, New York, NY 10011-4211, USA
10 Stamford Road, Oakleigh, Melbourne 3166, Australia

© The Economic History Society 1992

The Population History of Britain and Ireland 1500–1750
first published by The Macmillan Press Limited 1992
First Cambridge University Press edition 1995

Printed in Great Britain at the University Press, Cambridge

A catalogue record for this book is available from the British Library

Library of Congress cataloguing in publication data

Houston, R. A. (Robert Allan), 1954–
  The population history of Britain and Ireland 1500–1750/ prepared for
the Economic History Society by R. A. Houston.
    p.   cm. – (New studies in economic and social history)
  "First Cambridge University Press edition 1995" – Verso t.p.
  Includes bibliographical references and index.
  ISBN 0 521 55277 X (hc). – ISBN 0 521 55776 3 (pb)
  1. Great Britain – Population – History. 2. Ireland – Population –
History. I. Economic History Society. II. Title. III. Series.
HB3583.H63   1995   95–18507
304.6'0941–dc20   CIP

ISBN 0 521 55277 X hardback
ISBN 0 521 55776 3 paperback

DAMAGED

CE

For D.C.C., T.C.S. and E.A.W.

Contents

Tables

Note on references

References in the text in brackets are detailed in the Bibliography.
The author's name and date of publication are followed, where
necessary, by the page numbers in italics.

Author's preface

Population history is a large, complex and expanding area of research. For the non-specialist, unfamiliar terms, copious statistics and convoluted arguments also render it one of the most potentially confusing. Awareness of these potential difficulties explains the aims and layout of this pamphlet. Readers will not find a flat exposition of different points of view. Debates and uncertainties have been made explicit but the problem of synthesising substantial quantities of complicated material make it essential to differentiate possibly significant areas of disagreement from pointless bickering. Tables have been kept to a minimum. Population totals are discussed only briefly because structures and trends, and the reasons behind them, are more relevant to social and economic historians. The implications of demographic structures and trends are dealt with in passing. References in square brackets may indicate that an outline of the argument under discussion can be found in the work cited, not that its author necessarily espouses the viewpoint. Certain technical terms may require fuller explanation than can be offered in the text. Readers should consult Roland Pressat's *Dictionary of Demography*, a new edition of which has been prepared by Christopher Wilson (1988).

R. A. HOUSTON
Department of Modern History
University of St Andrews

Introduction

Most histories of Britain are histories of England. The quality of information about Scotland, Wales and Ireland is generally far inferior to that about England before the nineteenth century. Abundant sources and a well-established tradition of genealogy and of local social and economic history have made English historical demography more advanced than Scottish or Irish. The existence of specialist research bodies, notably the Cambridge Group for the History of Population and Social Structure, founded in the 1960s, has given population history a firm grounding. With the publication in 1981 of *The Population of History of England, 1541–1871* by two members of the Cambridge Group, England's demographic history moved onto a different plane. For that reason, England is treated as a benchmark in this book, a relatively well-documented and fairly well-studied country with which its near neighbours can be compared. Scotland, Wales and Ireland are not less interesting or important: far from it. They are simply less well researched.

Before *The Population History of England* a number of local studies of population, economy and society existed and some attempts at a general interpretation had been made. Working in the 1950s and 1960s, J. D. Chambers, M. Drake, D. Eversley and H. J. Habakkuk made the greatest contribution to English historical demography at this time, K. H. Connell to Irish. More sophisticated methods such as family reconstitution (see Chapter 2) were being developed in France by L. Henry during the 1950s and P. Goubert's magisterial 1960 study of *Beauvais et le Beauvaisis* is acknowledged as a landmark. With much 'fact' disputed and various theories of population dynamics in competition, *The*

1

Population History of England set out to provide a comprehensive interpretation from scratch. A similar attempt had been made in 1977 by M. W. Flinn and his collaborators (mostly T. C. Smout and R. Mitchison for the seventeenth and eighteenth century sections) in *Scottish Population History from the Seventeenth Century to the 1930s*. Serious source problems and some unfortunate methodological assumptions made this overview less satisfactory. Irish historians have followed up Connell, checking and reworking his findings. Efforts at synthesis have been confined largely to articles which struggle with difficult sources, outline population trends and speculate cautiously on dynamics (Goldstrom and Clarkson, 1981; Daultrey, Dickson and Ó Gráda, 1981).

The early modern period witnessed no 'demographic revolution' of the kind which transformed European fertility in the later nineteenth century (partly through the dissemination of effective contraception), or the large improvement in adult life expectancy during the last 50 years (partly through better medical care). In many ways, the sixteenth, seventeenth and eighteenth centuries were very different from modern times. Most noticeably, in the early modern period expectation of life at birth was half what it is in late twentieth century Britain. In others, such as the relatively late age of first marriage and the prevalence of small, simple families it is easier to identify with them. However, the centuries between the end of the middle ages and the dawn of the industrial revolution clearly command attention. They saw wars and invasions in Britain and Ireland as elsewhere in Europe but they also witnessed the demise of plague as a serious killer and, in some areas, of short-term mortality crises related to famine and disease.

There were important similarities between certain aspects of family and demography in Britain and Ireland, aspects they shared with much of north-western Europe (Hajnal, 1983). However, there were equally significant regional and perhaps 'national' differences in the way elements of the demographic system fitted together. The ancient parts of the early modern British Isles and Ireland had very different social structures. Despite a trend towards political and legal assimilation, and towards cultural integration, significant differences remained even in 1750 and we should not be surprised to find these reflected in demographic behaviour (Houston and Whyte, 1989). Both trends and the reasons behind them varied considerably between regions of the British Isles. Historical demographers now doubt if there was such a thing as a 'European demographic system', and except at a simple level there was no common demographic regime across England, Wales, Scotland and Ireland between 1500 and 1750.

The aim of the next section of this pamphlet is to discuss sources for early modern demographic history and the ways of exploiting them. Population structures and trends are then outlined before the dynamic components of fertility, nuptiality, mortality and migration are discussed. A substantial chapter on the relationship between demographic behaviour and its economic and social context concludes the pamphlet. Approximately equal space is given to Scotland and Ireland, where possible. On some topics, such as nuptiality, relatively more attention is given to these areas because of the need to outline sources, methods and explanations which have received little attention in existing literature. Yet, with the best will in the world there is no making up for the absence of sources and research for Scotland and Ireland. It is possible to present the facts for England and to discuss competing interpretations, though readers should not infer from this that English sources are absolutely reliable. For Scotland and Ireland it is more a question of trying to establish the facts and then conjecture about explanations. Wales is mentioned only occasionally.

1
Sources and methods

Sources

Two principal types of source are used by historical demographers. The first is records of ecclesiastical events – baptisms, marriages and burials. The second is listings of all or part of a local population drawn up for religious, military or fiscal reasons. Unfortunately, the sources used by historians of population were almost never compiled for strictly demographic purposes. Furthermore, interpretation of these sources is complicated by the ecclesiastical, administrative and legal differences between England and other parts of the British Isles. Hampered by suspicion and evasion, secular institutions had less access to reliable information than the church but the latter's interests were even further removed from the concerns of modern demographers than those of the flimsy early modern state. Human frailty compounds problems of omission: early modern numeracy was questionable, age-rounding to, say, multiples of 10 years was common, and reported ages may have been under- or over-stated according to circumstances. Source problems are much more serious than for nineteenth and twentieth century demography (Wrigley, 1966; Willigan and Lynch, 1982). We should be wary of early modern sources and adopt a degree of agnosticism about the results derived from them. We need to know whether the data are *reliable* – consistently measured – and *valid* – meaningful indicators of the concepts we wish to explore.

Except briefly during the 1650s, England had no civil registration until 1837, Scotland until 1855 and Ireland until 1864. The first national census was not conducted until 1801 (to all intents and purposes not until 1821 for Ireland). In the absence of these basic centralised sources for modern demography, early modern historians rely primarily on parish registers. In 1538 Thomas Cromwell, Henry VIII's famous minister, ordered that all parishes in England should keep records of baptisms, marriages and burials. Some parishes obeyed immediately but others took decades before commencing registration. Some registers were kept only intermittently and incompletely, others have not survived the ravages of damp, rodents, fire or carelessness. The Cambridge Group has more than 500 parish register counts for England. Parish registers can be supplemented by other sources. From 1629, for example, the London bills of mortality give yearly deaths from various causes in 130 city and adjoining parishes.

In Scotland, types of source are broadly similar. Edinburgh's Greyfriars' burial ground had an official keeper of the register from 1658, paid by the town council, and both Edinburgh and Glasgow have well-kept bills of mortality for the first half of the eighteenth century. These documents are especially welcome in view of the poor quality and survival of many Scottish parish registers. In common with much of Europe, Scotland's baptism and marriage records began earlier than those for burial, and those burial registers which were kept tend to under-record the deaths of infants and children; those they do record are sometimes denied even a name. Some parish registers began to be kept during the 1550s and 1560s but are few before the seventeenth century and those which survive are rarely complete (Flinn, 1977, *46–8*). For the upland areas of northern and western Scotland, the Highlands and Islands, statistics are almost wholly absent until the eighteenth century, a serious shortcoming in view of tantalising suggestions that this region, like seventeenth century Ireland, possessed rather different nuptiality patterns from the Lowlands (Houston, 1988, *19*; Ó Gráda, 1979). In some respects, the quality of Scottish registers is superior to that of English. Women kept their maiden name after marriage and are identified by it in baptismal and, sometimes, burial registers. This makes record linkage of baptisms less ambiguous than where the father only is mentioned since a statement of relationships to the living makes it easier to link deaths to earlier events. Burials of those unable to pay mortcloth dues (for hire of the pre-burial winding sheet) and clerk's fees are noted 'poor' in the better-kept registers, allowing analysis of socially-specific mortality in famine years such as 1698.

Similarly with Ireland, our understanding of pre-census demography depends on a handful of comparatively well-kept parish registers and listings of inhabitants conducted for taxation, military or ecclesiastical reasons. For Ulster, the registers of the established (anglican) church of Ireland are the best kept before the nineteenth century (Macafee, 1987). Approximately 100 Irish catholic registers survive for the eighteenth century but most state only names at baptisms and marriages, and most relate to towns in the east of Ireland. The seventeenth century is a wasteland as far as catholic registers are concerned – only those of Wexford town survive and are currently being analysed. Many protestant (church of Ireland) registers were destroyed by fire in 1922. In Wales too, survival and quality of registers is poor – though no worse than in Scotland or Ireland – and there are none in the Cambridge Group's sample. Projects are afoot in Ireland and Scotland to study elite genealogies, though these are typically much more informative about males than females. Lack of consistently and accurately recorded vital events seriously limits the statistical techniques which can be applied to sixteenth and seventeenth century Scottish data.

Even when parish registers survive, it is not always certain what proportion of vital events they record. Some 'marriage' registers are in fact lists of the couples whose banns were proclaimed but who may have married later or not at all. Changes in fashion could have a marked effect on registration. Clandestine marriages (not celebrated in accordance with the requirements of the established church) may have accounted for a sixth of all marriages among those born in 1666, but a generation before or after, levels of 4–5 per cent were more common (Schofield, 1985b, *14*). A similar trend is clear in early eighteenth century Scotland when, in the Edinburgh area at least, clandestine or 'irregular' marriage was fashionable. The main problem is that parish registers record ecclesiastical rather than vital events (Smout, 1981). If, for example, baptism was delayed there is a chance that infants who died very young would not be recorded. Fortunately, in Scotland the interval from birth to baptism was short during the second half of the seventeenth century and the first half of the eighteenth century. For example, 93 per cent of children in Haddington

1653–8 were baptised within a week, 94 per cent of Kilmarnock infants 1740–51. For England the interval is slightly longer – though not damagingly so until the late eighteenth century – and there was considerable variation between baptismal customs in different parishes.

Urbanisation had less of a detrimental effect on registration than is commonly assumed, at least before the later seventeenth century. London registers between 1580 and 1650 'are of a high standard of accuracy' (Finlay, 1978, *112*). This can be established by various methods. One, developed by the French demographer Bourgeois-Pichat, allows the extent of under-registration of infant deaths to be measured by comparing the numbers of children recorded as dying ('from birth trauma, congenital defect and functional inadequacy' – endogenous causes) during the first weeks of life with what is biologically likely (Schofield and Wrigley, 1979, *73*). All other deaths are caused by environmental or 'exogenous' causes. If this 'biometric' analysis shows levels of endogenous mortality to be too low then the register from which the figures were derived is probably defective. It also helps to know the number of stillbirths and, since there was no statutory require-ment to register stillbirths before 1927, any register which contains plausible numbers is likely to be generally well-kept.

Religious divisions were similarly less serious before the second half of the eighteenth century than is sometimes claimed. In England, under-registration caused by withdrawal from the an-glican church varied geographically but is estimated to have increased generally over the eighteenth century. Dissent flourished more noticeably in England than in Scotland and from the 1640s in London religious fragmentation and the growth of sects affected registration (Finlay, 1978). The spread of English dissent in the period after the restoration of the monarchy of 1660 was particu-larly rapid. The effect of religious differences on Scottish registra-tion was not significant until after 1689–90. For example, the small numbers of Independents in the 1650s and Quakers in the 1660s seem to have been prepared to present their children for baptism in the established church in the city of Aberdeen. Political and military problems, for example in the collection of the hearth tax, were more serious in the 1690s in areas sympathetic to the ousted Stuart dynasty. In early eighteenth century Edinburgh those

attending Episcopalian meeting houses, as opposed to the Presby-
terian kirks, were still supposed to register deaths with the keeper
of the city's mortality register. The number of communicants
attending the established church in one densely peopled central
Edinburgh parish remained constant from the 1730s to the1770s,
implying an acceptance of its offices.

For one religious group, distinctive practices have proved bene-
ficial to the historical demographer. Quakers did not baptise their
children, therefore all entries in the records of their monthly
meetings are of births. In addition to registers of vital events,
Friends kept family genealogies. What is more, Quakers only pass
out of observation because of death, because they left England or
because they had ceased to be Quakers rather than because of
moving from a parish (Eversley, 1981, *58–60*; Landers, 1990, *35–
6*). This makes family reconstitution easier and makes it possible at
all for Ireland where early parish registers are rare and in England
at times when anti-clericalism, non-conformity and clerical laxity
seriously limit the value of anglican registers.

The second main source of demographic information is the
listing of inhabitants. Listings which provide the ages of household
members are a particular boon to historians because techniques
are available to estimate mean age at first marriage, age gap
between spouses and the age of servants – all important demographic indicators. The first reliable and complete English age
listing is for the then rural parish of Ealing (Middlesex) in 1599.
The only reliable listings for Scotland before the mid eighteenth
century relate to urban communities and even these lack the detail
and comprehensiveness of their English counterparts. A 1755
'census' of Scotland carried out by Alexander Webster in connection with his work on clerical pensions has been extensively used as
a benchmark for population totals and, more recently, to provide
other demographic statistics (Mitchinson, 1989). Webster's dili-
gence in collecting, analysing and presenting these figures does not
bear too close an examination. For Wales there are several partial
listings of indeterminate quality, notably those for St Asaph's
diocese in northern and central Wales during the 1680s. These,
along with hearth tax schedules, have received little attention.

Where more than one listing of inhabitants survives during a
period of a few years, it may be possible to estimate the extent of

population turnover between the dates. The movement of vagrants and apprentices has been extensively studied from the records of the former's punishment and the latter's indentures (Clark and Souden, 1987). More detailed figures about geographical mobility by age, status and gender can be gleaned from the biographical details furnished by those who gave evidence before the church courts of England, from settlement certificates (introduced in England from 1662) and from Scottish 'testificates' issued by the church to movers (Clark, 1979; Houston, 1985). Voluntary and involuntary movement of British people to the New World can be studied from convict transportation records, contracts of indentured service, port records and passenger lists (Galenson, 1981; Ekirch, 1987).

Methods

Ways of exploiting these sources have become increasingly sophisticated in the last three decades. Traditional approaches used contemporary estimates of population, such as those of Gregory King or William Petty; or documents showing the number of communicants or taxpaying households which were then inflated by a suitable multiplier to give total population; or multiplying baptism or burial totals by a constant birth or death rate to give a total for a parish. The first national exercise of this kind was carried out by John Rickman, director of the 1801 British census. Rickman used aggregates of baptisms, burials and marriages from sample years to estimate population totals in 1570, 1600, 1630, 1670, 1700 and 1750. This method provides approximate figures for English population but it is imprecise, open to criticism and tells us little more than total numbers. Birth totals cannot be subjected to a single multiplier because changes in the age structure of fertile women mean they are not constant; deaths rates too vary according to age structure and type of environment. The problem with communicant lists such as those of 1563 or the famous Compton 'census' of the 1670s is estimating the age at which communion took place, the proportion of the population not included, and the extent of religious non-conformity. Population listings generally cover only one age group, geographical area, occupation or religion. Alldridge's valuable study of Chester, using parish rate (local tax) books and listings highlights the problems. One projection of the population in 1692 is 34 per cent lower than that for the same year using a different source (Alldridge, 1986, *122–7*).

Contemporaries could be highly perceptive and well-informed but they could also be selective in their use of evidence and inaccurate in their conclusions. The famous novelist and journalist Daniel Defoe overestimated London's early eighteenth century population by a factor of two. The way in which contemporaries collected quantitative material is sometimes frustratingly unclear. Arthur Dobbs wrote of northern Ireland in 1725: 'From several returns made to me of the number of persons in each family, in a great many contiguous parishes in the county of Antrim, I find the medium to be 4.36 to a family' (Clarkson, 1981, *22*).

For Ireland and Scotland, serious source deficiencies mean that traditional methods continue to be used, albeit in a more sophisticated way, though Macafee and Morgan have shown that partial family reconstitution can be done with eighteenth century Ulster registers (Morgan, 1976; Macafee, 1987). Daultrey *et al.* (1981) have tested Irish hearth tax schedules and have been able both to distinguish between data of widely differing reliability and to identify the main regional trends in the better series. Attempts to identify and explain structures and trends rely heavily on comparisons with better documented historical populations and on the creation of more or less plausible scenarios. Scottish and Irish demographic history before the nineteenth century, like Dutch, 'emphasizes the investigation of macrodemographic questions in a regional context' and depends on 'resourceful use of flawed and imperfect data' (De Vries, 1985, *661*). As De Vries points out for the Netherlands, fertility, nuptiality and mortality rates are 'based largely on fragmentary and indirect evidence. Any general statements should be thought of as hypotheses awaiting confirmation rather than as the conclusions of systematic research' (1985, *663*). Some use has also been made of population theory as a way of defining aims and content. These theories are best seen as a set of hypotheses to be tested rather than moulds into which historical data are to be crammed. What follows should be treated as a set of 'controlled conjectures' based on sporadic and imperfect evidence, especially as far as Scotland and Ireland are concerned. Because absolute proof is difficult to establish, historical demographers may have to eliminate the impossible or create likely parameters of the possible.

There is still merit in traditional approaches, especially when documentation is suspect or too fragile to bear the weight of demanding methods. However, these approaches have increasingly been complemented, and indeed superseded, by new methods which allow more accurate quantification of a wider range of demographic variables. Population totals at different dates are useful but without an idea of what produced them we cannot go much further. Family reconstitution and aggregative analysis help us to understand why population changed and how it was made up.

Family reconstitution involves amassing all the information about vital events in individuals' lives. Numbers of family genealogies are created which can then be analysed to calculate demographic measures such as the age at first marriage, the number of children from every 1,000 born who died before the age of one year (infant mortality rates), and the number of children a woman bore between marriage and the end of her fertile period. The technique is appropriate only to parishes with well-kept registers and even then is better suited to some than others. Family reconstitution is possible for London though the high level of geographical mobility and small parishes means that age at marriage, age-specific marital fertility and adult mortality cannot generally be calculated because age at marriage, at the birth of children and at death are unknown. By contrast, record linkage is easier and more productive in a large rural parish like Cartmel in north-west England since mobility can occur without people moving out of observation. Parishes whose inhabitants share a small number of surnames cannot be reconstituted because it is frequently impossible to link vital events accurately – a common problem in Wales.

Because of the strict rules governing the linking of names in family reconstitution, only a minority of the population of a parish can be used for some demographic measures (Wrigley, 1966). In English studies completed to date, age-specific marital fertility rates use just 16 per cent of legitimate live births because mothers have to be born locally for their ages to be known. High levels of geographical mobility mean that adult mortality is also based on small percentages of the total population. Between a third and a half of those born in an English parish also married and died there, in contrast with France where nearly four-fifths did so. Infant mortality rates, on the other hand, are based on roughly 80 per cent of legitimate live births (Wrigley and Schofield, 1983, *158*). Family reconstitution is much more representative than is sometimes asserted. For example, the fecundability of women excluded from age-specific marital fertility calculations is the same as those on whom the statistics are based. And studies which have followed movers over parish boundaries – and therefore out of observation in conventional reconstitutions – have found close similarities with stayers. However, mobility creates a bias – specifically, a 'censoring effect' – of which we must be aware. While movers and stayers may have the same age-specific vital rates, those who marry latest and those who survive longest have most chance of escaping inclusion in age at marriage and adult mortality estimates because they are more likely to have moved.

Family reconstitution sets rules of observation which defines the population at risk and therefore offers census-like information on delineated subsets of the population without full census data. It details the dynamics behind population trends. However, it is time consuming, localised and provides small numbers of events from which to generalise. Recent publications use data from just 13 English parishes (Wrigley and Schofield, 1983). For Scotland, full family reconstitutions have proved difficult though some partial ones are available for a handful of parishes and recent work on Fife promises to produce more usable statistics from this method. In order to obtain a broad picture of demographic development, another technique has been used.

Aggregating monthly or annual totals of baptisms, marriage and burials has a long pedigree stretching back to Rickman in the early nineteenth century and before (Wrigley, 1966). These aggregative analyses formed the model for Wrigley and Schofield in their magisterial *Population History of England* (1981, *15–154, 195–9*). First, a new sample of 404 parish registers was drawn from the nearly 10,000 English parishes. The quality and coverage of these was checked and adjustments made to ensure that the sample, though not random, was as representative of size, geographical location, social structure and ecological type as possible. Baptisms, marriages and burials were inflated into national series, including an adjustment for London, and then these ecclesiastical events were converted into vital rates by applying demographic models to make allowances for under-registration of births, marriages and deaths at different periods. Armed with a known age structure in 1871 and a set of life table estimates of the age structure of mortality, it is possible to step backwards, five years at a time, by making each age-group five years younger and adding those estimated to have died or emigrated in between. This technique, 'back projection', gives population totals, age structures and net migration estimates every five years back to 1541. These can be used to calculate growth rates as well as measures of fertility, mortality and nuptiality (Schofield, 1985a, *583–4*; Trussell, 1983, *307–10*; Flinn, 1982, *450–1*; Gutmann, 1984).

Both methods and results have provoked criticism, scepticism and sometimes even hostility. Review articles by Flinn, Gutmann, Henry and Blanchet, and Trussell are particularly helpful on technical aspects. While an important part of the *explanation* of changing population depends on flawed estimates of wages and prices (outlined in Chapter 6 below), discussion here is confined to possible problems in Wrigley and Schofield's *description* of population size, structures and trends. One concern is over the number and distribution of parishes. Aggregative analyses from 530 parishes were whittled down to the 404 which form the core of the study in the years 1662–1812. But, the further back in time, the fewer parishes are included: just 45 at the starting date of 1541 (Flinn, 1982, *448–9*). What is more, an eighth of all parishes in the sample are from Bedfordshire, none at all from Cornwall. That the four northernmost counties provide just 13 parishes (3 per cent of the sample) is a serious defect in view of the possible similarities and differences between Scottish and English demography.

Criticisms have also been made of aspects of the methodology. Estimates for 1541–1630 are particularly tentative because plausible numbers of births and deaths for the 95 years before 1541 have to be 'invented' in order to create a 1541 population (Henry and Blanchet, 1983, *807–10*). The weakest links in the chain are the migration estimates which are residuals and depend on questionable assumptions about continuities in the age structure of emigration (Guttmann, 1984, *15–16*). This issue is dealt with by Oeppen (1991), who shows that the fluctuations in net migration estimates are an artifact of the statistical method originally used in Wrigley and Schofield (1981). However, Oeppen also finds that the total volume of migration is the same 1541–1866 and that the effect on population totals is negligible. Henry and Blanchet (1983, *815–18*) draw attention to the large margin of error in estimates of proportions never married over time but allow that the trends identified by Wrigley and Schofield are probably correct. Summing up the main strain of criticism, Flinn opined: 'readers will note with some apprehension the enormous distance between the raw data and the final levels and rates' in *The Population History of England* (1982, *457*).

Yet, we should not allow these clouds of criticism to obscure the merits of back projection, population modelling and other statistical and theoretical tools. The methodologies have the great advantage of being rigorous and open to scrutiny and replication. Those who read through the 700-odd pages of *The Population of History of England* will be impressed by the intellectual effort involved, by the clarity of the exposition, and by the willingness to acknowledge potential shortcomings in data and findings. Those who have tried alternative assumptions and projections – for example, vital rates before 1541, age structures of mortality, under-registration at different periods – have been impressed by the sturdiness of the results (Henry and Blanchet, 1983). By identifying and allowing for deficiencies in the sources Wrigley and Schofield offer a much higher standard of transparency and accuracy than earlier work. The results have an internal consistency which is encouraging in a subject where context is everything. The pooled data on fertility and mortality available from the 13 reconstituted parishes are, for example, close to those achieved by back projection. Indeed, many of the criticisms levelled at the authors are answered by Wrigley and Schofield in the new preface to the 1989 edition of *The Population History of England*. Their publications since 1981 have used constructively some of the alternative suggestions raised by their critics. It seems fair to concede the authors' claim that 'the main outlines of the population history of England seem to be remarkably robust in the face of quite large errors or uncertainty in the data' (1989, *xvi*).

The latest demographic tool to become available is computer microsimulation. Programs such as CAMSIM randomly assign characteristics in accordance with assumed distributions based on demographic probabilities. This creates model populations which can be used to estimate the chances that, for example, a father is survived by one or more sons (Laslett, 1988). This is useful in discussing the role of inheritance in family formation. Another possibility is to estimate the numbers of eligible husbands available for the remarriage of widows, indicating whether remarriage chances were determined by demographic or cultural and economic factors. Microsimulation is particularly useful for modelling kin universes which are almost impossible to recreate by conventional methods. Family, career and business strategies could also be influenced by changing demography. For instance, young women in England around 1800 had twice as many living cousins as in 1700 (Laslett, 1988, *15*). With microsimulation, studies of historical demography may be entering a new phase of development which promises to address a host of hitherto inaccessible problems.

2

Structures and trends

When population estimates were merely an obligatory backdrop to more 'important' topics such as politics, religion and warfare, historians concerned themselves almost exclusively with overall numbers. Estimating population size from scratch is, in fact, a more difficult exercise than when the demographic parameters are known. The size and composition of a population are, after all, a direct function of fertility and mortality, and are indirectly influenced by nuptiality and migration. Nevertheless, an idea of population structures and trends can set the stage for an analysis of the motors of change.

For England, robust figures exist for five-year intervals beginning in 1541. Those used here are from Oeppen (1991) and are very slightly higher than those presented by Wrigley and Schofield (1981, *528–9*) because a more reliable statistical technique was used on the data. The main reason for the adjustment is a different set of net migration estimates (see Chapter 5). England had some 3.02 million people in 1541, a figure which rose almost without interruption to reach 5.47 million in 1656. Thereafter a period of stagnation or slight decline set in. Population did not exceed the 1656 level until the 1730s but then grew at a modest rate to reach 5.90 million in 1751 and more rapidly to 8.70 million by 1801. Population growth rates peaked at just under 1 per cent a year in the third quarter of the sixteenth century and at their lowest a century later were − 0.25 per cent. Between 1541 and 1751 yearly growth rates averaged under 0.5 per cent.

These trends can be explained almost wholly by changes in fertility, measured by the gross reproduction rate (GRR), and mortality, of which expectation of life at birth (e_0) is a good overall indicator (see Pressat, 1985, for these and other definitions). Proportional changes in these two measures will be equally important in changing the intrinsic growth rate (r) (Wrigley and Schofield, 1981, *228–48*). There is no reason to believe that one is inherently more powerful than the other. For the period 1571–1611 fertility and mortality were stable, combining to give an intrinsic growth rate of 0.85. During the following 60 years fertility fell and mortality rose in equal proportions to produce a fall in r. The main factor in population growth 1671–91 was fertility while between 1691 and 1751 mortality exerted the most significant impact. How and why fertility and mortality changed, and the contribution of migration to population trends, are discussed in Chapters 3–5.

Estimates of total population in Ireland and Scotland rely mainly on taxation records. Multiplying the number of households, hearths or taxpayers by a suitable figure gives population totals. The trick is in identifying the relationship between a house's physical characteristics such as the number of hearths and the number of inhabitants. Surviving schedules of the 1691 tax on hearths levied in Scotland show 2 hearths per household in Edinburgh, just under 1.5 in the rest of the Lowlands and 1.2 in the Highlands. Allowance must be made for legitimate exemption and evasion. The second variable is the proportion of the total households which paid tax: the range is 60–67 per cent here. We also need to know the average size of a house. Using figures from the 1790s and assuming no change in household size over the eighteenth century, mean household size was roughly 4.5, ranging from less than 4 in Clackmannan to nearly 6 in Sutherland. Finally, if we assume that the areas without surviving hearth tax returns had the same ratio of population to those with extant schedules as they do in Webster's 1755 census, we can estimate the population of Scotland at 1.23 million in 1691. This is 3 per cent lower than in 1755 and implies a miniscule growth between the dates. A period of serious mortality in the 1690s when population fell by perhaps 10–15 per cent was followed by half a century of modest growth of perhaps 0.3 per cent a year, comparable with that of contemporary England (Tyson, 1992).

Earlier estimates for Scotland are largely conjectural, though it may be possible to identify periods of change. Population growth seems to have been fastest in the late sixteenth and early seventeenth century, if we can judge from indirect, unsystematic and possibly subjective literary sources. There is no evidence of serious pressure of population until after *c.* 1570 and the balance of probability is that famines, wars and disease kept growth rates low between the early fourteenth century and the mid sixteenth. Poverty, for example, was not as apparent as in English and European towns for much of the century. However, legislation in 1574, 1579 and 1592, coupled with contemporary comments, create the impression of prevalent vagrancy and begging. The real wages of Edinburgh labourers fell sharply from the 1560s, confirming the pressure of population on resources.

Scotland experienced similar growth rates to Ireland's average of 0.2–0.4 per cent a year 1687–1755 though with marked short-term fluctuations. Numbers in Ireland stagnated from 1687, when the first reasonably reliable hearth tax returns become available, until 1706. Strong growth, touching 2 per cent a year, followed in most counties until the famines of 1727–9, 1740–1 and 1744–6 dampened it down (Dickson *et al.*, 1982, *156–75*; Daultrey *et al.*, 1981, *622-7*). The difference became even more marked thereafter, with Ireland's population growing at three times the Scottish rate 1755–1801. Moving backwards in time, Cullen and others have presented some ingenious political arithmetic for the seventeenth century (Cullen, 1981, *90–4*). Cullen believes that numbers may have doubled between 1600 and 1712, with fluctuations in growth rates mainly caused by changes in immigration: fastest growth came 1600–40 and 1652–9. Irish growth rates in the seventeenth century were much faster than either England or Scotland (Clarkson, 1981, *25–7*). Ireland in 1500 was probably lightly populated and experienced less growth than other areas of Europe in the sixteenth century. The best recent estimates of Irish population are approximately 800,000 people in 1500, one million in 1600 and 2 million by 1687. There were slightly less in 1700 but perhaps 2.4 million in 1750 and 5 million by 1800. These figures should be treated with extreme caution. Eighteenth century sources for Ireland are treacherous enough but those for the seventeenth are like quicksilver and earlier estimates almost purely conjectural.

Irish population was more directly affected by war than Scottish or English. The towns of Armagh and Galway were devastated in the early sixteenth century and the ruthless Elizabethan conquest and plantation of Munster may have caused a regional fall in population, against the European trend. There were further dislocations during the 1640s and 1650s, including the storming of Drogheda and Wexford, and in Ulster 1689–91. In parts of Ulster these upsets and the end of rapid immigration reduced nuptiality and fertility dramatically in the first half of the eighteenth century compared with *c.* 1660–89 (Morgan, 1976, *13–14*; Cullen, 1975). Dickson claims that these wars 'cancelled out the natural increase of many years' (1988, *97*). However, wars were not the only factor: regional population trends were closely related to wider economic and political circumstances (Macafee and Morgan, 1981).

Within these national pictures there were marked local and regional variations. Certain types of community grew more quickly than others. 'Open' parishes with ample pasture and opportunities for industrial work tended to experience the fastest increases. Areas of the Cambridgeshire fens and of north-west England saw rates of growth in the Elizabethan period double those of Norfolk and Suffolk (Smith, 1978, *228*). In the north of England during the eighteenth century mining and industrial communities mushroomed. However, there is no guarantee that particular types of community will experience growth. Husbands warns against ecological determinism while arguing that 'proto-industrial' and urban communities were the real engines of growth in south-east England between the 1520s and 1670s (Husbands, 1987). Kussmaul shows that this was even more so in the following century (Kussmaul, 1990, *142–4*). Numbers could fall as well as rise within a region. The most buoyant Scottish region 1691–1755 was the western Lowlands with 12 per cent growth, the least so the north-east Lowlands where population fell by 6 per cent.

Throughout Britain and Ireland, towns of 10,000 or more grew faster than the population as a whole from the mid sixteenth century (Table 1). A threshold as high as 10,000 is needed because of the difficulty of distinguishing smaller urban centres in the sources though there are also positive reasons for choosing it (Wrigley, 1985). The rate of change varied over time and may be linked to changes in real incomes. The largest Scottish towns in 1500 – traditional provincial centres – also headed the hierarchy in

Table 1 *Proportions living in towns of 10,000 or more and total population of those towns in thousands*

	Scotland		England		Ireland	
	000s	%	000s	%	000s	%
1500	13	1.6	80	3.1	0	0
1550	13	1.4	112	3.5	0	0
1600	30	3.0	255	5.8	0	0
1650	35	3.5	495	8.8	17	1.1
1700	53	5.3	718	13.3	96	5.3
1750	119	9.2	1021	16.7	161	7.0
1800	276	17.3	1870	20.3	369	7.4

Source: Whyte, 1989a, 22.

1700: Edinburgh, Glasgow, Aberdeen, Perth, Dundee. Comparisons between tax assessments in 1639 and 1691 show that, except for Edinburgh and Glasgow, many of the larger towns experienced declining population though other smaller centres did grow. The fastest rates of increase probably occurred in the small towns which proliferated in this period (Whyte, 1989a, *26*). Even in 1700 Scotland's largest city, Edinburgh, had no more than 40,000 inhabitants and probably closer to 30,000 though the figure depends on what parts of the metropolis are included. Dublin grew quickly from around 20,000 in 1650 to 130,000 in the 1750s, becoming the second largest town in the British Isles but with only a fifth of London's population. Cork was the second largest Irish city with 12,000 people around 1650 and 70,000 inhabitants in the mid eighteenth century.

English urbanisation before the eighteenth century was dominated by London. The metropolis was 13 times larger than the second biggest city (Norwich) in 1600, 19 times larger in 1700 (Wrigley, 1985, *686*). London's multiple advantages as court, port and capital city help to explain its dramatic growth and a share of national population – 5 per cent in 1600, 11.5 per cent in 1700 – without parallel in contemporary Europe. London's share of England's population more than doubled in the sixteenth century and nearly doubled again 1600–1700. London had to draw in 900,000 immigrants between 1600 and 1700 to grow from 190,000 to 550,000, and by doing so consumed 80 per cent of the natural increase in England's population. Other English towns fared less well in the sixteenth century leading some scholars to speak of an urban crisis. However, old established provincial centres, ports, and new leisure and industrial towns flourished after *c.* 1660. Bristol had about 21,000 inhabitants in 1700, 50,000 in 1750 and Liverpool more than trebled in this period to 22,000 in 1750. The growth of towns like this accounts for nearly all the doubling of proportions urban 1670–1800 (Wrigley, 1985). English urbanisation was a reflection of, and a stimulus to, agricultural improvement and the expansion and diversification of industry and commerce.

Vital events in large towns followed different seasonal patterns from rural areas. In the countryside, marriages peaked in April and May in pastoral parishes, in September and October in arable ones, following the rhythms of the agricultural year. Conceptions also tended to be clustered in the slack agricultural seasons. Mortality followed a similar seasonal pattern to baptisms, clustering in January, February and March. Towns (and rural industrial parishes) had a flatter curve through the year for all vital events (Wrigley and Schofield, 1981, *288, 293, 299*; Kussmaul, 1990). Population turnover peaked at the main hiring fairs of Whitsunday and Martinmas. These patterns prevailed in Scotland and Ireland too.

Other superficial similarities are apparent between regions of the British Isles. Taxation schedules and communion rolls indicate that mean household size in Lowland Scotland was comparatively small at between four and five people; composition was simple (Flinn, 1977, *196*; Tyson, 1985, *125–6*). Household formation depended on the north-west European norm of economic independence, at least in the Lowlands. In other respects, such as the preponderance of females in the population, and the higher proportion of female-headed households in towns as opposed to rural areas, Scottish households are unexceptional in a north-west European context (Houston, 1979; Tyson, 1988). Eighteenth century English observers were inclined to believe that Irish households were larger than English but Clarkson suggests they may have been of similar size (1981, *20–4*).

Finally, we can consider age structures. Demographers and economists conventionally present age distributions in terms of dependent versus productive members of the population. Those aged 14 years or less and those aged 60 and above are viewed as net consumers of resources, those 15–59 either self-supporting or net producers. Fortunately, these conventions correspond with the most significant indicators of population composition. A country with relatively high fertility will have a younger age distribution than one with low fertility. Between 1541 and 1751 the proportion of English population aged 60 and over changed little: the lowest figure (just over 7 per cent) was in 1566, the highest (just over 10 per cent) 1716. The proportion aged 14 or under peaked in 1556 at nearly 37 per cent; the lowest proportion of children came in 1671 – just under 29 per cent (Wrigley and Schofield, 1981, *443–50, 528–9*). The point to note is that while the age structure is 'young' compared with modern western countries, it is nothing like as imbalanced as some developing countries where children may account for more than half the population. A relatively light 'dependency burden' has important implications for the balance between population and resources, and thus for the standard of living of all age groups.

The only semi-reliable estimate of age structure in contemporary Scotland is given in Webster's 1755 census. Even he was forced to make assumptions, from the clergy's returns which he used, about the age structure of those too young to be examined on the catechism (Mitchison, 1989, *71*). Webster's figures are likely to be far less precise than ones derived from back projection for England but they indicate perhaps a quarter of the population aged 10 years or less and just over two-fifths aged 20 or less. If we can lay any weight on these estimates, the population age structure was not very different from contemporary England. Reporting of advanced ages in historical populations is often seriously inaccurate and proportions elderly are not offered here. The age structure of the Irish population was probably younger than that of England or Scotland because (as we shall see in Chapter 3) of its high, fertility-dominated growth rates *c.* 1600–1750.

Describing population structures and trends is valuable in itself. To explain them we must analyse different combinations of mortality, nuptiality, fertility and migration.

3
Nuptiality and fertility

The medieval and early modern church made it extremely easy to marry. Boys could marry at fourteen, girls at twelve throughout Britain, except between 1653 and 1660 when England's civil marriage ordinance raised the minimum age of consent to sixteen and fourteen years for males and females respectively. Until 1753 in England (and much later in Scotland and Ireland) there were four different paths: an exchange of oaths before witnesses, an exchange of statements of intent to marry followed by sexual intercourse, a licence from the church authorities dispensing with banns, and church marriage preceded by the publication of banns. With rare exceptions, the bulk of England's population, and probably also those of Scotland and Ireland, waited some ten years after puberty before marrying. Only one English bride in eight was a teenager when she first married 1600–1749. The reasons for this are discussed in Chapter 6. The present section is concerned with the effects of decisions to marry or remain celibate, to reproduce within or outside wedlock. It is almost wholly concerned with women since their reproductive behaviour is much more significant to population dynamics than that of men.

Nuptiality

Until the 1960s many historians believed that women married relatively early in the past. Partly, they based their ideas on literary evidence and partly on elite social groups. Unless backed up by other evidence, contemporary writing may provide a distorted view of social behaviour. It has also been clear that until the end of the seventeenth century the aristocracy behaved completely differently from ordinary people in their marriage patterns. Women of the British peerage usually married as teenagers and only two out of every five remained unmarried at age 20. Their husbands were aged 22–24 years: five or more years older (Hollingsworth, 1964).

The technique of family reconstitution has provided new figures on the nuptiality of ordinary men and women. Between 1600 and 1799 family reconstitutions for 13 English parishes generate estimates of mean age at first marriage for women. Figures for 1550–99 cannot be given because the late start of many parish registers truncates the population in observation and thus biases age at marriage downward. The 13 parishes cover a wide range of ecological types from an isolated pastoral community (Hartland, Devon) through a commercial agricultural village (Terling, Essex) and a textile centre (Shepshed, Leicestershire) to a large market town (Banbury, Oxfordshire) (Wrigley and Schofield, 1983, *158–9*). Results are presented in Table 2.

Changes in age at marriage are important for the following reason. In populations with natural fertility (see below), fertility is largely a function of age and is highest in the twenties when women produce approximately 0.4 live births a year on average. Given prevailing adult mortality, a union will produce about four live births. Therefore, if age at first marriage rises or falls by one year, the total fertility of a marriage will change by approximately 7 per cent. When age at marriage falls, women begin bearing children younger which, in addition to increasing total fertility, shortens the mean length of generation and thereby accelerates population growth.

In the age of the industrial revolution, changes in the age at marriage dominated changes in fertility attributable to nuptiality. However, the numbers of women who remain celibate throughout their reproductive careers also has a powerful impact on total fertility. For all its merits, family reconstitution has little to offer on the proportions who never marry. Aggregative back projection fills the gap. For women born before the middle of the eighteenth century this other influence on nuptiality, celibacy, was far more important. Some 5 per cent of those born around 1566 never married by the end of their childbearing span (i.e. before the 1610s) but among the cohort born in 1616 22 per cent remained celibate. Some explanations of changes in nuptiality are offered in

Table 2   *Mean age at first marriage for men and women in 13 English parishes (by marriage date)*

	Men	Women
1600–49	28.1	25.6
1650–99	28.1	26.2
1700–49	27.2	25.4
1750–99	25.7	24.0

Source: Wrigley and Schofield, 1983, *162*.

Chapter 6. For the present, it is worth noting that changes in the proportions of women never married did not occur at the same time as changes in age at first marriage for women, and that until the early eighteenth century changes in celibacy dominated the movement of fertility (Goldstone, 1986, *10–11*; Weir, 1984; Schofield, 1985b).

Some tentative estimates of age at marriage and proportions never married in Scotland are available. Mean age at marriage derived from statements about age and marital status among a thousand court deponents shows a mean age at first marriage of 26–27 years for Lowland adult women giving evidence 1660–1770 and celibacy to the end of the fertile period of at least 11 per cent (Houston, 1990, *63–6*). The age at marriage figure finds support from partial family reconstitutions of two parishes. One is the Highland community of Laggan where age at first marriage for women born before 1800 was approximately 27–30 years (Flinn, 1977, *279*). The other is the large parish of Kilmarnock in the mid eighteenth century where just 57 women have been traced at birth and marriage. Those living in Kilmarnock town married at a mean age of 23–24 years, rural women at 26–27. Preliminary results from a study of eighteenth century Fife indicate an age at first marriage for women in the mid-20s. Permanent spinsterhood in a sample of west central Lowland and western Border parishes was comparatively high at perhaps 20–25 per cent (ignoring extreme figures) (Flinn, 1977, *276*, *280*). Taking 11 per cent as a minimum and 25 per cent as a maximum, these figures are broadly comparable with late seventeenth and early eighteenth century England. They imply a substantial constraint on overall fertility. However, they seem to have been less variable in the long term than in

England. Mean age at first marriage for Scottish women stayed at 26–27 during the later eighteenth and first half of the nineteenth century while in England the range was 23–27. Celibacy too remained high in Scotland (Houston, 1988, *19*). There is some unsubstantiated literary evidence of early marriage in the western Highlands and Islands (Flinn, 1977, *279*).

For Ireland, the most reliable nuptiality and fertility figures relate to Quakers. Eversley compares these systematically with English Quakers, and contends that Irish Friends' demographic behaviour was different from their Irish catholic or protestant counterparts in degree rather than in kind. Irish Quaker women married earlier and had shorter intervals between births than English Quakers (Eversley, 1981, *64–5*). Mean age at first marriage for Quaker women 1650–99 was 22.7 years and 23.2 for 1700–49. Their husbands were four and a half years older in both periods. This distinguishes Irish Quakers from their rural counterparts in southern England. Women first married there at 24.9 years 1650–99 and 26.3 years 1700–49; their husbands were 28.6 and 28.1 years old respectively. Irish Quaker women started reproducing at a younger age and in their most fecund years.

Other estimates reinforce this picture. Among 121 marriages in the church of Ireland registers for the linen weaving parish of Killyman in Ulster 1771–1810, mean age at first marriage for women was 22 years, for males 26 years; half the women were married by their 21st birthday (Macafee, 1987, *152, 155–6*). An even lower figure of 18 or 19 years for women is offered for Blaris, Lisburn in the late seventeenth and early eighteenth century though there are serious source problems here and a censoring effect in the family reconstitution which would lower mean age at first marriage (Macafee and Morgan, 1981, *56*).

Literary evidence lends weight to the picture of relatively early marriage in Ireland. Sir William Petty and other observers believed that 'Irish women marry upon their first capacity' and noted a stress on the fertility of unions apparently not found in England (Ó Gráda, 1979, *285*). Petty had local knowledge of Dublin and Kerry, and was better informed than most contemporaries who followed a derivative and cavalier tradition of writing which based images of Ireland less on personal observation and empirical enquiry than on literary conventions and ethnocentric cultural prejudices about *all* non-English societies – specifically, that the women would enter the loose bonds of marriage while still young, would be naturally fecund, and would bear large numbers of children with ease.

Recent work by David Dickson lends credence to the idea that seventeenth-century Irish women did marry for the first time at a comparatively early age but firmly within the bounds of the north-west European marriage pattern (Dickson, 1990). Listings from county Dublin and Munster in the 1650s contain a substantial proportion of unmarried female servants with a median age of 25–26 years, showing early and universal marriage cannot have existed. An estimate of age at first marriage can be made by subtracting the reported age of the first child listed from that of the mother then subtracting a further year to allow for marriage to first birth interval. A median age at first marriage for women of 22–23 years can be suggested which is consistent with the Quakers and the other estimates given above. At the same time, the age gap between spouses was wider than in England at slightly more than five years, implying that Irish men married for the first time in their late twenties. Ó Gráda concludes that 'in Ireland early marriage was the norm and age at marriage roughly constant long before' the eighteenth century (1979, *285*; Dickson *et al.*, 1982, *173–4*). It may also be that female celibacy was relatively low but marriage patterns were not those of eastern or southern Europe. What is more, the similarity between Quaker, church of Ireland and Irish catholic nuptiality indicates that the causes lie in economic circumstances rather than in the cultural behaviour of Ireland's indigenous population. This reinforces Eversley's picture of clear differences between English and Irish Quaker nuptiality (1981, *86*). Irish Quakers behaved in this way because they were Irish rather than because they were Quakers.

The age at which women first marry has a powerful impact on total fertility. Early first marriage probably explains much of the rapid and sustained population growth in Ireland during the seventeenth century and again in the eighteenth century. However, it has been estimated that in late sixteenth century England 25–30 per cent of all marriages were remarriages. This figure fell over time to reach 10 per cent in the mid nineteenth century. Divorce was difficult and expensive to obtain; most unions were ended by death or, occasionally, desertion. Contrary to expectation, only a small part of the reduction in remarriages was related to a fall in adult mortality. The likelihood of being bereaved depended on mortality, that of remarrying on social or economic circumstances. Problems of source and method make analysis of remarriage from family reconstitutions difficult. Just 423 widowers and 295 widows can be studied from the available reconstitutions; the market town of Gainsborough provides half the widows and two-thirds of the widowers while 70 per cent of cases come from the eighteenth century (Schofield and Wrigley, 1981). Of those whose age at remarriage is known, nearly a half of widowers and just over a third of widows remarried within a year though the mean interval nearly doubled or both sexes between the late seventeenth and late eighteenth centuries. Age at bereavement was not a significant influence on remarriage chances but the more dependent children a man or woman had the longer he or she would wait to remarry.

To a limited extent, changes in the composition of the population could affect nuptiality. By moving into towns as servants and apprentices, young adults had their marriages delayed by formal or informal means. One girl in ten aged 15–24 would have been working in one of the four main Scottish towns at the end of the seventeenth century (Whyte and Whyte, 1988, 97). Imbalances between young men and women may have had a similar effect. London-born girls could expect to marry younger than their immigrant peers in the Elizabethan and early Stuart period but a century later growing sex imbalances among the nubile population made it harder for young women there and in other large towns to find a husband.

Legitimate fertility

The most striking features of English marital fertility are its comparatively low level, its stability over time and its homogeneity across space. The total marital fertility ratio varied just 1 per cent above and below its 1600–1799 average in different half centuries (Wrigley and Schofield, 1983, 169). Unpublished work by Christopher Wilson shows a marriage to first birth interval of approximately 19 months in 16 parishes 1550–1749. The interval for all subsequent births was 31 months; both figures were stable over the two centuries. Fecundability (the probability of a woman conceiving in one menstrual cycle) and fecundity (the physiological capability of a couple to produce a live birth) can vary – in response to changes in nutrition or health, for example – but it is almost impossible to investigate these changes in historical populations. The prolonged, debilitating malnutrition needed to change fecundity in closely studied modern populations was unlikely to have been present in early modern Britain. Those women exposed to the risk of starvation would probably have been among those too poor to have married anyway. The most potent influence on marital fertility was infant-feeding practice. Mothers who breastfed their children tended to wait longer before conceiving another child – and gave their infants a much better chance of surviving to reach their first birthday. Marriage order affected fertility 'almost entirely in a substantially reduced fertility of widower/widow remarriages' (Schofield and Wrigley, 1981, *225*).

For Ireland, we must again use the Quakers and patchy local studies to represent the population as a whole. Quaker morality forbids pre-nuptial fornication and all recorded births were legitimate. Age-specific marital fertility was consistently and appreciably higher for Irish Quakers than for southern rural English Friends for all age cohorts, 1650–1749. Birth intervals were clearly shorter for Irish Quakers than English, except after five or more children had been born. In particular, marriage to first birth interval 1650–1749 was 6–7 months less than English Quakers at about 15 months and 4 months less than Wilson's estimate (Eversley, 1981, *65*, *72–3*). Subsequent birth intervals were shorter for English than Irish Quakers (25 months compared with 27–28 months) but both are less than Wilson's 31 months. Completed family size was larger too for Irish Quakers: just under 7 compared with just over 4 for southern English Quakers and just over 5 from English family reconstitutions (Wrigley and Schofield, 1983, *176*; Eversley, 1981, *76*). For late eighteenth century Killyman, Ulster, Macafee reports marriage to first birth intervals of about one year and subsequent intervals of 24–30 months (1987, *157*). Sterility increases with age but the figure of 10 per cent of married couples who are involuntarily sterile found by Eversley for Irish Quakers appears to be average for early modern populations (1981, *79*). If, as seems likely, Quakers are representative of the bulk of the population, Ireland's comparatively low age at first marriage and high marital fertility in the seventeenth and early eighteenth century were powerful forces behind population growth compared with England's.

The short marriage to first birth interval among Irish Quakers finds similarities with that among a small sample from the town of Kilmarnock in Scotland. The marriage to first birth interval was 13.3 months 1730–53 compared with 15.9 months for Irish Quakers, 19.9 for southern English Friends 1700–49, and about 19 months for 16 English parishes 1550–1749 (Flinn, 1977, *287*). Taking all higher birth orders together, intergenesic intervals at Kilmarnock were almost identical to English Quakers and slightly above Irish. If Kilmarnock is at all representative of Scottish marital fertility, the similarities with Ireland are intriguing. Total marital fertility would also have been higher in Scotland than in England, balancing out some of the effect of higher Scottish mortality (see below). One reason for the shorter birth intervals in Ireland compared with England may be the higher fecundity of women there – as contemporaries claimed. Another explanation might be that breastfeeding was less extensively practised by Irish Quakers though this cannot account for the shorter marriage to first birth intervals. We might also expect that infant and child mortality would be higher among children weaned earlier but there is no clear evidence of this except among Irish Quaker children aged 1–9 years and then only 1700–49 but not 1650–99 (Eversley, 1981, *80*). Kilmarnock aside, we can say nothing useful about Scottish marital fertility before the late eighteenth century. However, pronounced regional variations in both legitimate and illegitimate fertility during the nineteenth century are again fascinating. If carried back into earlier centuries they would contrast strongly with England's relative homogeneity.

There is virtually no material on overall Scottish fertility before the eighteenth century. Tyson's reasonably reliable estimate of the crude birth rate for Aberdeenshire 1691–5 is 29 per 1,000 (1985, *126*). Mitchison offers a higher rate of 35 per 1,000 for Scotland as a whole based on Webster's 1755 census age structure and model life tables (1989, *71*). Both estimates are significantly lower than Hollingsworth's very approximate 41 per 1,000 in the 1750s – a figure which is hard to square with other nuptiality and fertility parameters (Mitchison, 1989, 66). They are, however, close to the English levels of 32 per 1,000 in the 1690s and 33 in the 1750s.

Potentially, a woman might have up to 30 children during her childbearing span between the ages of roughly 15 and 45: assuming no breastfeeding or severe mortality among the newly born. There are prominent historical examples of large families and high fertility but these are unusual. One seventeenth century English clergy-man's wife, Elizabeth Walker, bore 11 children during her life while Charles I's queen Henrietta Maria produced seven children between autumn 1628 and spring 1639. Putting children out to wetnurses, a practice among elements of the upper classes, ex-plains the latter example. But even in 'reference' communities with no deliberate birth control the average maximum number of live births by the end of a woman's reproductive career is under nine, the average birth interval is approximately 30 months, and the actual maximum birth rate around 50 per 1,000. Because of relatively late marriage, breastfeeding, and biological factors women in such communities are only pregnant for a sixth of their reproductive years (Bongaarts, 1975). The most potent factor in controlling total fertility was nuptiality.

Whatever their desires, couples do not seem to have limited the number of children born to them. In particular, 'parity-specific' birth control was not an option. In other words, parents could not decide to have a set family size and then achieve just that number. It was possible to space births by practising primitive contraceptive methods such as abstinence or withdrawal, or by increasing the length of time a child was breastfed and thereby inhibiting (if not absolutely preventing) conception. The age pattern of marital fertility in a natural fertility population is determined largely by physiology. If family limitation is practised, fertility will fall more rapidly with age and rising parity. Demographers use a measure (m) of the difference between a 'natural' fertility regime and one in which contraception is practised to indicate birth control. A m value of less than 0.2, characteristic of seventeenth and eighteenth century English marital fertility, means that no parity-specific birth control was being used. Other telltale signs are absent from England. If a notion of parity exists there will be a replacement effect as women whose children have died will continue childbearing longer in order to replace them. No such effect has been found for 1600–1799 and indeed Wilson concludes that 'while the existence of family limitation in pre-industrial England cannot be ruled out, it is highly unlikely that it was of any significance in determining the overall patterns of marital fertility' (Wrigley and Schofield, 1983, *169–70*; Wilson, 1984, *240*).

Nor is there any clear evidence that parents sought to maximise the number of children they had, either as a way of increasing the family labour supply or securing for their old age. For one thing, children in both Scotland and England tended to leave home just as they were becoming most productive (in their mid-teens) and to use their earnings from working as servants and apprentices once they had left home to establish economic independence and set up their own household rather than remitting money to their parents (Kussmaul, 1981). Labour needs were met by hiring strangers rather than kin. For another, help for the aged and infirm was mainly provided by the community rather than by family members in England with no guarantee that parents could rely on their offspring for support, though this may have been expected. In Scotland the role of family and neighbourhood support and of informal charity was probably greater than in England but there is no evidence of a stress on fertility or of a desire to have a large family for practical reasons. In any case, high levels of geographical mobility militated against kin-based support, at least in the Lowlands. There is, however, evidence of Highland seasonal workers and domestic servants, working in the Lowlands, remitting to the home family in the later eighteenth century.

Illegitimate fertility

Most births took place within marriage. However, a 'procreative career' may begin before marriage and persist after the death of the last spouse; it may even exist within marriage but not with the spouse, difficult though it is for demographers to identify this in the past. Births outside marriage have attracted considerable attention from historians because of their implications for social life and personal relations (Laslett *et al.*, 1980). Yet, while pre-nuptial conception was quite common, at least in England, bastardy was not.

The ratio of illegitimate births to all births in 98 sample parishes rose in the last quarter of the sixteenth century to peak at 3.4 per cent in the early 1600s. Bastardy ratios fell thereafter to reach a nadir of 0.9 per cent 1655–9 before beginning a steady rise to reach 3.1 per cent 1750–4 and 5.3 per cent in the early 1800s (Laslett *et al.*, 1980, *14*; Wrigley, 1981, *157*). Trends in pre-nuptial pregnancy followed a similar path. In 16 parishes with well-kept registers, 31 per cent of legitimate first births were conceived within eight months of marriage 1550–99, 23 per cent 1600–49, 16 per cent 1650–99 and 22 per cent 1700–49 (Laslett *et al.*, 1980, *23*).

Bastardy is often treated as a pathological phenomenon or as an indicator of changing moral standards. Its recording is a function of the perceptions of church and community, its definition clouded by different interpretations of what constituted a marriage. For those born around 1666 roughly 14 per cent of marriages were 'clandestine' (not celebrated in accordance with the requirements of the established church) though 4–5 per cent is more usual for seventeenth and early eighteenth century England (Schofield, 1985b, *14*). However, historians now believe that most English bastard-bearers were ordinary women who decided to begin having sex in anticipation of marriage, conceived but then became the victims of social and economic dislocations or personal misfortunes which prevented them marrying. This would explain the late sixteenth century rise in illegitimacy which came at a time of serious dearths and of pressure of population on a relatively inelastic economy. An explanation predicated on an economic downturn is less obviously successful in accounting for the long rise in illegitimacy from the mid seventeenth to the early nineteenth century, during which period conditions were generally buoyant. The trough of the 1640s and 1650s was more the result of under-reporting by neighbours and officials in response to draconian penalties introduced during the English revolution rather than a sign that puritan morality had been accepted by the populace (Laslett *et al.*, 1980, *158–91*).

Legitimate and illegitimate fertility can be seen as elements of the same social practice: both marital and extra-marital births were the result of a market in procreative unions. Courtship intensity varied over an individual's life and this may explain why illegitimacy levels in England tended to change with general fertility levels, why having a bastard did not prevent subsequent marriage, why trends in illegitimacy and pre-nuptial pregnancy moved together, why there was apparently an inverse relationship between age at first marriage for women and bastardy ratios, and why the age when women bore bastards was close to age at first birth within marriage (Laslett et al., 1980, 467–9).

Bastardy ratios were higher in Scotland and also less changeable. Illegitimate births were roughly 4 per cent of all births 1660–1750. A similar proportion of legitimate first births were conceived before marriage –much lower than in England (Mitchison and Leneman, 1989, 164, 168). There were marked regional variations even in the late seventeenth century. In aggregate, the relatively low levels mean that the effect on overall fertility was slight. Nationally, there was a slight downward trend 1660–1750 in both illegitimacy and pre-nuptial pregnancy but levels were more stable than in England. This finding lends further weight to the idea that nuptiality and fertility varied much less in Scotland than in England c. 1660–1750. The social background of illegitimacy was also different from that of England. Scotland may have possessed two distinct groups of extra-marital procreators: one intending marriage who began to have sex before marriage and another who did so without any strong prospect of marriage. The reasons for this, and their significance, are not yet clear (Mitchison and Leneman, 1989, 176). The low level of extra-marital sexual activity has sometimes been attributed to the action of a strong brand of protestantism working through parish 'courts' called kirk sessions. The differences between Scotland and England may also be related to sources, those for Scotland causing historians to underestimate pre-nuptial pregnancy though it is hard to believe that the marked divergence between the societies can be wholly explained in this way.

Illegitimacy was low in Ireland during the eighteenth century. Among the few figures available, Macafee cites 2 per cent bastardy among anglican births at Loughgall, county Armagh, 1707–29. In the second half of the eighteenth century three catholic parish registers reveal illegitimacy of less than 3 per cent and pre-nuptial pregnancy of about 10 per cent (Connolly, 1979, *8*, *18–19*). Much more work is needed but it may be that early and more general marriage thanks to easier economic conditions removed some of the reasons for illegitimacy. The Counter-Reformation may have brought about changes in sexual practices and other aspects of behaviour during the seventeenth century but it would be too simplistic to relate low illegitimacy solely to the influence of the catholic church.

4
Mortality

For most age groups, levels of mortality in early modern Britain were much higher than in the nineteenth and twentieth centuries. Mortality could vary explosively in the short term in local areas. As many as a quarter of the population might be carried away by spectacular bouts of disease and famine during a two to three year period. Individual parishes had their own rhythms of mortality with huge local variations in the pattern and timing of fluctuations (Dobson, 1989a, *280*). Charting those patterns provides important insights into the reasons for mortality trends and fascinating detail about their social and economic significance. But the main task facing the historical demographer is to establish the overall level of mortality which tended to vary much less at regional and national levels.

Mortality crisis

The main text on Scottish population history sees mortality as the principal motor of demographic change before the nineteenth century (Flinn, 1977). This interpretation follows a historiographical tradition which stresses the significance of violent, short-term fluctuations in death rates for overall mortality. Flinn and his collaborators relied principally on inference from these short-term trends. Population grew 'naturally' because of a surplus of births over deaths but growth was periodically curbed by bouts of severe mortality caused by famine and disease. 'Mortality in the seventeenth century tended to fluctuate violently in the short run, and there is little doubt that it was primarily the changing pattern of mortality fluctuations that determined whether population would grow, stagnate or decline' (Flinn, 1977, *4*).

Irish historians have been more cautious about linking mortality crises to underlying death rates. But, as Clarkson remarks, 'the Malthusian spectre hangs heavily over popular perceptions' thanks to memories and folklore of the severe famine of the 1840s (1988, *220*). Certain periods witnessed serious crises, most notably that of 1740–1 which may have killed a quarter of a million people and there were other periods of famine in the 1620s, 1640s, 1650s and 1720s (Clarkson, 1988; Gillespie, 1988, *77–89*). The 1740–1 famine, occasioned by abnormal weather, simultaneous failure of all foods and lack of imports due to shortages abroad, led to destocking of farm animals, abandonment of farms and widespread vagrancy (Dickson, 1988, *97, 103–4*; Post, 1985).

Short-term mortality indices can certainly be used to identify periodic crises which were a distinctive feature of early modern Britain and Europe. Scotland and Ireland seem to have experienced mortality crises at different times from England and until later in their histories. Mortality crises had important social repercussions and could exert a powerful short-term influence on demographic and economic trends. Perhaps a fifth of the population of Aberdeenshire may have died during the crises of the 1690s (Tyson, 1986, *50*). However, there are a number of problems with an argument which relates short-term mortality crises to overall levels of mortality over long periods. Some shortcomings can be demonstrated by reference to English and European experience, others on more methodological and theoretical grounds. Part of the explanation for variations in mortality may be statistical. Most English parishes were small and there would have been large random variations in vital events from year to year. Half the parishes in Kent, Essex and Sussex in the seventeenth century had less than 200 inhabitants (Dobson, 1989b, *399*). Scottish parishes tended to be larger but random variations cannot be ruled out. Scottish figures should also be treated with caution since recording of deaths was rarely consistent or complete and periods of high mortality may have encouraged more diligent registration. In some cases 'surrounding years' may be only one or two each side of the crises. Even in a run of high mortality, experience was very varied, some areas being unaffected, others suffered once, certain locations frequently. The worst hit areas of Scotland in the famine of 1697 was the north-east, in 1699 the south-east. In England, France and Spain during the sixteenth and seventeenth centuries chronologies of growth and stagnation are not necessarily linked to mortality crises (Souden, 1985, *239–40*). Crude death rates may move down when the incidence of crises increases, as in late sixteenth century England.

Overall, it seems unwise to equate evidence of mortality fluctuations or crises with overall levels of mortality, population trends or mechanisms of change. Peaks in mortality in some years do not mean that mortality over time was high except in the very short term. England's population fell by more than 5 per cent between 1556 and 1561 as the crude death rate soared to over 50 per 1,000 in 1557. Expectation of life during the 5-year period centred on 1556 was roughly 15 years or a third less than that for the quinquennia 1551 or 1561 (Wrigley and Schofield, 1981, *230, 234*; Oeppen, 1991). However, the crises of the late 1550s were only a 'blip' in the steadily rising e_0 and hardly dented strong population growth. The significance of the underlying mortality and fertility regime is shown in the effects of the 1690s' dearths in Scotland. The slow growth of 1700–55 was almost certainly a continuation of a relatively high mortality and low fertility regime which existed in the seventeenth century. Famine and disease reduced total numbers in the 1690s but had no lasting effect on growth rates in the long term. As Souden reminds us, 'there is not a necessary relationship between moving totals of deaths and medium-to-long-term measures of mortality, between variance and level' (1985, *234*). These and other methodological problems were recognised by Flinn and his collaborators but were largely ignored in formulating their interpretation. It may be that mortality is the main dynamic variable in Scottish population history and the principal reason why population did not rise very quickly over the long term. But there is little reason to believe this on the evidence presented.

Levels of mortality

The principal difference between mortality patterns in the twentieth century and those in the seventeenth is that a much higher

Table 3 *Infant and child mortality in 13 English parishes (rates per 1,000) and expectation of life at birth in years (e_0) among the whole population (both sexes)*

	$_1q_0$	$_4q_1$	$_5q_5$	$_5q_{10}$	e_0
1600–49	161.3–162.3	89.3	41.2	25.2	36.4
1650–99	166.7–169.7	101.5	40.0	24.2	33.9
1700–49	169.2–195.3	106.5	40.6	22.8	34.5
1750–99	133.4–165.5	103.5	33.2	20.7	36.5

Source: Wrigley and Schofield, 1981, *252–3*; 1983, *177*.

percentage of all deaths occurred amongst the young in the past. Table 3 gives the most recent (and robust) estimates for England from 1600 onwards. Infant and child mortality come from family reconstitution studies, expectation of life at birth (e_0) from back projection estimates. The figure $_1q_0$ is the number of deaths among infants below one year of age per 1,000 live births. The other quotients relate to child age groups. A range is given for infant mortality because under-registration has to be taken into account. Life expectancy at birth of England's population was higher than in contemporary Europe (and Scotland) partly because infant and child mortality was relatively low. An earlier study showed that infant mortality in eight English parishes fell 1550–99 to 1600–49 but that of children aged 1–4 rose sharply and of 5–9-year-olds even more so (Schofield and Wrigley, 1979, *67, 95*). The fall in expectation of life at birth between the first and second half of the seventeenth century was caused by a rise in early child mortality, the eighteenth century rise by improving infant mortality.

Variation in infant and child mortality between different types of community was enormous. Infant mortality in the market town of Gainsborough (Lincolnshire) was three times the level of that in the coastal parish of Hartland and child mortality between five and nine years old was double. The role of infant and child mortality in determining total life expectancy is striking. Expectation of life at birth in a relatively 'healthy' parish like Hartland may have been as high as 50 years 1600–1749 compared with just 30 years in Gainsborough (Wrigley and Schofield, 1983, *179*). In wealthy central London parishes 1580–1650 expectation of life at birth was roughly 35 years but in the poorer suburban and riverside parishes with large numbers of incomers the figure was nearly a third lower (Finlay, 1981a, *107–8*). The worst non-urban infant mortality was found in marshy coastal and estuarine parts of south-east England where water-borne infections and malaria created levels of 250–300 per 1,000 (Dobson, 1989a, *265*).

Quoted life expectation at birth of, say, 35 years does not mean that everyone died at that age. Once a person had survived infancy and childhood they could expect to live through several decades of adult life. Men who became London freemen in the mid sixteenth century, at an average age of about 26 years, could expect to live a further 28 years (Rappaport, 1989, *69*). Between 1550 and 1749 male expectation of further life at age 30 among reconstitution populations was 28.4 years at its worst (1650–99) and at its best 30.4 years in the first half of the eighteenth century (Wrigley and Schofield, 1981, *250*). Women's life expectancy was almost identical. Adult life expectancy varied much less than infant or child over time and most changes in expectation of life at birth (and most geographical variations) are attributable to changing mortality of those aged 10 or less.

Historical demographers must again extrapolate from Irish Quaker mortality to that of the population of Ireland as a whole. Age-specific adult mortality of English and Irish Quakers was similar 1700–49. There was little to choose between infant mortality 1650–1749 or that of children 1650–99 but Irish Quaker child mortality at ages 1–9 was much higher than English 1700–49. Infant and child mortality among southern rural English Quakers was slightly better than that among English family reconstitution populations, possibly because unhealthy market towns are included in pooled data for the 13 parishes. For infants and children as well as adults there was little improvement in Irish Quaker mortality until the nineteenth century, though more recent work has suggested a fall in mortality in parts of Ulster from the mid eighteenth century (Eversley, 1981, *80*; Macafee, 1987, *146*).

Expectation of life at birth was apparently lower in Scotland than England. Using the age structure given in Webster's 1755 census and model life tables, Mitchison has calculated a life expectancy at birth of 31 or 32 years compared with 36 or 37 for England (Mitchison, 1989, *71*). Much of this difference was accounted for by different levels of infant and child mortality – infant mortality of over 220 per 1,000 compared with 170–190 in England 1700–49 – though adult mortality was also higher in Scotland (Wrigley and Schofield, 1983, *177*). The crude death rate for Scotland was 31 per 1,000 compared with 26 for England in the 1750s.

There is evidence of increasing adult life expectancy among elite Edinburgh-based lawyers ('advocates'). The period 1650–1749 saw an important fall in adult mortality similar to that occurring among certain European elites. Expectation of life at age 30 among advocates entering their professional association 1650–99 was 27.4 years compared with 33.9 years 1700–49 (Houston, 1991). These figures relate to adults from a privileged elite. Mitchison (1989, *71*) has estimated expectation of life at age 30 of 25.8 years for both sexes from Webster's 1755 census age structure and model life tables. This means that adult life expectancy for advocates was at least a third better than for the population at large. In Scotland there may have been wide divergences in the mortality of social groups of a kind well documented on the Continent – notably in seventeenth century Geneva – but not apparently found in England at so early a date. Expectation of life at birth among British peers was lower than for the population at large during the seventeenth century, only slightly better 1700–49 but clearly superior in the second half of the eighteenth century (Hollingsworth, 1964, *56*).

Differences between the mortality of social groups are strongly related to living conditions. Plague, for example, was no respecter of status once caught but those who lived in well-built brick houses had much less chance of being infected by rat fleas than poorer people who inhabited crowded and inferior dwellings. Whether differential mortality also highlights social attitudes is much less clear. It has been claimed that infant and child mortality rates obtaining in early modern Britain show that children were not valued. This view can be challenged on a number of fronts. First, there is now overwhelming evidence from diaries and autobiographies to show that parental affection was not new to the eighteenth century. Second, urban poor relief provisions and regulations governing servants and apprentices clearly demonstrate the value placed on the health of children and youths, albeit partly for economic reasons (Houlbrooke, 1984, *127–56*; Wrightson, 1982, *104–18*).

More sinister is the possibility that female infants and children suffered greater neglect than male (Wall, 1981; Finlay, 1981b). Wall thinks that higher female infant mortality after a number of births to a family is at least suggestive of differential neglect in some parishes. Yet, the evidence is far from conclusive. In fact, a study of eight English parishes 1550–1749 found that there was a slight, 'normal' surplus of male infant and child deaths compared with female. Far more important than sex to life chances was parental wealth with poorer children more likely to die young than those from better-off backgrounds. Most important of all was environment: infants and children living in congested and insanitary communities had high mortality (Finlay, 1981b, *70–1, 76;* Wall, 1981, *136–7*). Mortality differences were a direct result of living conditions and infant-feeding practices, and an indirect effect of levels of wealth. Finally, there is intriguing evidence for England that infant mortality was high for first births, much lower for second, third and fourth births, but rose sharply for higher birth orders (Wrigley and Schofield, 1983, *180–1*).

If the demographic experience of urban dwellers differed from their rural counterparts growing urbanisation might have a significant effect on demographic trends by changing the composition of the population. Towns were, for example, significantly less healthy environments than rural areas. There were just 0.87 births for every death in London 1580–1650 (Finlay, 1981a, *59*). Infant and child mortality, already severe in early seventeenth century London, worsened in late century and continued to rise into the eighteenth century (Landers, 1990, *41–2*). Given urban/rural mortality differences, an increase in London's share of English population from 5 per cent to 10 per cent (as happened 1600–1700) would reduce national e_0 by one year (Wrigley and Schofield, 1981, *415, 472–6*). London and other towns certainly helped to restrict population growth in the later seventeenth century but the net effect of urban growth should not be exaggerated. The lower the starting level, the smaller the effect on national population of urban growth. The compositional effect of urbanisation on mortality, or nuptiality and fertility, would have been significantly less in England than in the Netherlands, where more than 30 per cent of the population lived in towns of 10,000 or more in 1600, the effect even more limited in Scotland and Ireland (De Vries, 1985, *666–7*).

Causes of death

Describing changing levels of mortality is difficult enough with intractable early modern sources. Explaining the observed structures and trends is considerably more of a problem. Parish registers only rarely give cause of death and their descriptions can confuse as much as they enlighten. Urban bills of mortality may be more forthcoming. In London, experienced but non-specialist 'searchers' cursorily examined a corpse and reported the reason for death to the clerk of the bills. Descriptions such as 'the pox' (smallpox) or 'a bloody flux' (dysentery) are readily identifiable, and the symptoms of bubonic plague hard to miss. But, among the 150 other descriptions used, 'fever' or 'dropsy' could be almost anything; 'blasted and planetstruck' is intriguing if nothing else (Galloway, 1985, *491*).

Yet, even where causes of death are not given it is possible to piece together a plausible explanation from indirect indicators because each disease has its own etiology and epidemiology. A time-consuming, if potentially fascinating, piece of detective work is to follow systematic differences in mortality patterns at a local level. For example, Dobson finds an extensive coverage of moderate mortality peaks in south-east England in the 1670s and 1680s covering all ecological and environmental types. Looking at the duration and seasonality of mortality, she identifies gastric diseases such as typhoid, dysentery and salmonella (Dobson, 1989b, *418–19*).

Another killer has been tracked down in south-west England. The very high death rates at Colyton between November 1645 and November 1646 suggest that a highly morbid disease was present. The mortality, perhaps a fifth of the population during that year, was confined to that parish and was probably not caused by an airborne infection which would have spread more widely. Its slow passage through the parish further indicated an insect-borne infection. Certain diseases tend to kill victims in particular age groups or at specific times of the year. Typhus kills mainly adults in the winter and is carried by human lice; dysentery spread by flies is a summer disease. Both can be ruled out for Colyton. Seasonality and the clustering of deaths in certain households show that plague was present (Schofield, 1977).

Plague is a high-profile disease which commentators were likely to record because of its symptoms and urban focus, and because of the fear it induced. But it was clearly not equally serious everywhere and its overall effect on mortality may have been less than is assumed. The last serious outbreak of plague occurred in Scotland 1645-9 when it may have killed as much as a fifth of Scotland's urban population (Flinn, 1977, *147*). However, less than 12 per cent of the population of seventeenth century Scotland lived in towns of 2,000 or more inhabitants and since plague was primarily an urban disease the effect on population totals may have been less severe than urban mortality figures and contemporary alarm suggests (Whyte, 1989a, *28*, *33*). The same point can be made for England. In 1604 the Durham mining parish of Whickham lost perhaps a fifth or a quarter of its population, a proportion comparable with the London epidemic of 1563. However, between 1580 and 1650 plague accounted for just 15 per cent of all deaths in London and the proportion of national deaths would have been lower still (Finlay, 1981a, *111–32*; Slack, 1985). The worst mortality crisis in early modern England was actually caused by the influenza epidemic of 1557-9. Plague's disappearance, from Scotland after the 1640s, and from England after the 1660s, may have been compensated for by other killers such as dysentery, measles, influenza or pulmonary complaints, while smallpox probably became endemic in parts of England and all over the Scottish Lowlands from the 1670s and 1680s (Flinn, 1977, *115*, *158*, *163–4*). If smallpox was truly a universal childhood disease in the eighteenth century this would distinguish Scotland (and Sweden) from England where it was mainly endemic in London.

Starvation is apparently well documented for certain periods such as 1596-8 or 1623-4. Yet, it is by no means certain that the main killer in famine years was hunger since the social dislocations upon which contemporaries remarked so forcibly may have increased the likelihood of catching morbid diseases (Walter and Schofield, 1989, *53–4*, *67–8*; Flinn, 1977, *179*). Sir Robert Sibbald wrote of the 1690s famines in Scotland: 'Everyone may see death in the faces of the poor that abound everywhere; the thinness of their visage, their ghostly looks, their feebleness, their agues and their fluxes threaten them with sudden death' (Flinn, 1977, *170–1*). In the spring of 1700 when the worst of the dearth was over, the

Scottish church ordered a token fast because of 'the great and unusual sickness and mortality throughout the land'. Famine mortality tends to affect extensive areas simultaneously, whereas disease mortality spreads slowly in a wave-like motion from one community to another. Starvation deaths usually occur close to the periods of highest prices, as in Munster 1740–1. Later mortality peaks are likely to be the result of disease epidemics. Typhoid and dysentery were killing people in Edinburgh in the autumn of 1741 when food supplies were returning to normal after the serious shortages of the previous harvest year (Post, 1985, *241–2*). Galloway believes that an increase in London deaths 1640–1750 among middle and older age groups in times of grain price surges was because they migrated into the city and died from diseases to which they had no immunity (1985, *500*). Other connections between nutrition and mortality are discussed in Chapter 6.

An allegedly common female experience was death in childbed. A woman who went through an average six or seven full-term pregnancies would run a 6–7 per cent chance of dying in childbirth. Maternal mortality accounted for a maximum of 20 per cent of all female deaths between the ages of 25 and 34, 11–14 per cent aged 20–24 and 35–44. To appreciate how little effect death in childbed may have had on women's attitudes, a large English village of 1,000 inhabitants, where a quarter were women aged 15–49, would experience only one maternal death on average every third year. Women must have been aware of the risks but may have seen them as distant. Maternal mortality in eighteenth century London was, however, 30–50 per cent higher than elsewhere in England. While the risks of dying in childbed were much greater for women than in the twentieth century, so too were those of dying from many other causes (Schofield, 1986, *259–60*). Finally, higher female mortality in the childbearing years should be set alongside higher male mortality in those years thanks to occupational risks – coal-mining accidents in north east England or plague deaths among south-east dock workers, for example.

Quantifying the relative importance of different causes of death is notoriously difficult. Landers shows that nearly a half of deaths among London Quaker children aged 5–9 were from smallpox and that this disease is important in accounting for the rise in child mortality in the early eighteenth century (1990, *54–5*). Ten times

as many deaths were attributed to smallpox as to typhus in the
London bills of mortality 1630–1730 (Appleby, 1975, *15*). The
number of deaths from typhus remained fairly constant over this
period but its relative significance as a killer decreased as the
population of the city more than doubled. Some 20 per cent of
reported deaths at Dublin 1661–1745 were attributed to smallpox
(Ó Gráda, 1979, *288*).

Different age groups were susceptible to different diseases. Jones
argues that the decline in infant mortality in rural north Shropshire
from the late seventeenth century was thanks to a reduction in
winter respiratory infections in the first three months of life. The
doubling in mortality of those aged 6–11 months 1711–60 was
mainly the result of smallpox, measles and other diseases (1980,
244–9). For contemporary London, Landers posits that gastric and
respiratory diseases particularly affected the under-twos while
smallpox and other infections were the main killers above that age
(1990, *58–9*). Substantial improvements in infant and child mortality did not begin until the second half of the eighteenth century
(Riley, 1987; Landers, 1990). It is probably safe to say that most
deaths in the early modern period were from infectious diseases
rather than from accidents, non-infectious ailments and old age as
in the twentieth century.

5
Migration

Historians once believed that population was essentially immobile before the economic changes and transport developments of the nineteenth century. Research in the last three decades has radically modified this perspective. Four out of every five witnesses before the church courts of Elizabethan Buckinghamshire said they had moved at least once in their lives. Over seventeenth century England as a whole, between a half and two-thirds of a parish's population would be renewed every 12 years. Between 1681 and 1686 approximately 40 per cent of household heads in parishes of central and north Wales had moved. Evidence from the Weald shows that better-off people moved shorter distances than the poor. An extreme example of this pattern was the mobility of vagrants: usually young, single males moving long distances in search of subsistence. Vagrancy was a crime punishable by whipping and return to parish of origin. Those caught in the south-eastern counties in the late sixteenth and early seventeenth centuries were drawn from all over England (Clark and Souden, 1987, *29–34*).

Important changes were taking place over time, with the mid seventeenth century representing a watershed. Improved economic conditions substantially reduced concerns about vagrancy in the second half of the seventeenth century and probably also long-distance subsistence migration itself. This was part of a wider trend towards less frequent, shorter distance and more formalised movement. In the diocese of Bath and Wells, lifetime immobility increased from a third of church court deponents in the early seventeenth century to a half in the later century. This change was, however, much less pronounced in East Anglia. Apprentice migration fields contracted dramatically and the system itself fell into decay. Between 1486 and 1750 the average distance travelled by provincial recruits to London companies was halved from 212 km to 111 km. The proportion of young men of known origin coming from the northern counties fell from 51 per cent 1486–1500 to 4 per cent in the 1740s while the share from London and the Home Counties grew from 28 per cent to 72 per cent (Wareing, 1980, *243–4*). Norwich and Southampton saw a 90 per cent reduction in the number of formal enrolments 1600–1700. Formal apprenticeship survived longer in the north of England and in Scotland but even here by the early eighteenth century it became increasingly confined to the wealthier trades and professions. Apprentices were becoming more local in their origins, as were agricultural servants whose movement was more institutionalised by the Settlement Acts after 1662. The later seventeenth century also saw greater seasonal mobility to meet the changing labour needs of a more specialised agriculture: for example, Welsh girls who came to work in the market gardens around London. In short, the sixteenth and early seventeenth centuries in England were characterised by 'a relatively ill-defined and undifferentiated system of migration. More basic, localised movement shaded into longer-distance travelling. Crude subsistence or push factors were a vital part of the migration matrix. Pull factors were not matched to the precise needs of the economy' (Clark and Souden, 1987, *32*).

Recently, the emphasis in research has switched from mobility towards stability (Boulton, 1987). Even in communities experiencing rapid growth by immigration, such as London in the late sixteenth and early seventeenth century or the contemporary mining parish of Whickham, there was a core of long-established inhabitants (Rappaport, 1989; Wrightson and Levine, 1989). This is not to deny the problems of assimilation for movers and host communities alike, or to question the existence of a high level of population turnover. It is to suggest that among certain (predominantly middling) sections of local communities there was considerable stability and continuity and that this has implications for the distribution of wealth and power within society.

Scotland shares many of the structures found in England. Geographical mobility within Scotland was extensive from an early date. The existence of servants in husbandry and a large land-poor class of 'cottars', both of whom moved frequently over short distances, coupled with the growth of towns and the evidence of extensive vagrancy from the later sixteenth century clearly indicate this. Population turnover occurred mostly among young, single people three-quarters of whom stayed less than three years in a parish; it was linked to the rhythms of agricultural life (Houston, 1985). Like England, most parishes would also possess a stable core. Some 45 per cent of completed tenancies in Angus (1650–1714) were less than five years long though 65 per cent of renewals were by sitting tenants (Whyte, 1989b). Taking into account adult mortality levels this implies a degree of permanence.

Most movement was local and over distances which people could walk in a day. Longer-distance migration involved apprentices and seasonal workers. Edinburgh was the only town with a truly national catchment area for apprentices in the period 1583–1700. Other towns had more localised recruitment areas and it was only in the early eighteenth century that Glasgow, on the way to becoming the largest Scottish city, began to make inroads into Edinburgh's appeal (Houston and Withers, 1990). Distances moved, and possibly population turnover as well, increased in eighteenth century Scotland. Vagrancy remained a problem well into the eighteenth century. Seasonal migration of Highlanders – who made up a third of Scotland's population in 1755 – to the Lowlands during the summer is documented from the later seventeenth century and may have existed before. Transhumance was practised on the Scottish Border in the sixteenth century but died out in the seventeenth (Kussmaul, 1990, *44*). Given the importance of geographical mobility, the presence of clear regional variations in illegitimacy, and the possibility of significant differences between Highland and Lowland demography, generalisations about 'Scottish' population (like Dutch) 'may obscure a series of distinctive regional demographic processes that were linked together by migration' (De Vries, 1985, *682*).

A similar suggestion has been made for England. The south-east and south-west differed substantially from each other in the extent of male and female migration, the sex ratio among movers and the proportion of local moves. A half of Devon's church court deponents in the seventeenth century were still living in the parish of their birth. This compares with a third of men and a quarter of women from Somerset and Wiltshire. Further east the proportions who never moved fell to a fifth of males and a sixth of females (Souden, 1987, *315–17*). There must also have been a net movement of males to the south-eastern counties (except London) and of females to the south-west because differences in the sex ratio at birth and burial in these regions are too large to fit observed demographic parameters. The spread of pastoral husbandry in the west of England during the late seventeenth century reduced the need for agricultural workers in general and for men in particular. Depopulation would follow unless industry was introduced to mop up the surplus labour (Kussmaul, 1990). Contrasting rates of regional population growth may be explained by differential migration. North Wales experienced faster growth *c.* 1550–*c.* 1670 than the south, possibly because of English immigration. Regional variations in Irish growth rates, notably the buoyancy of Ulster and Munster in the seventeenth century, may also be related to immigration from Scotland and England (Macafee and Morgan, 1981; Dickson *et al.*, 1982, *156–69*). The eighteenth century saw the beginnings of a substantial redistribution of population from the north to the central Lowlands of Scotland.

Most population turnover and seasonal migration had little impact on levels and distribution of people. Permanent movement, to towns or from one region to another, certainly did. Towns were unhealthy environments which needed large numbers of immigrants to maintain their populations, let alone sustain the growth apparent *c.* 1550–1800. The effect of migration on the population of Chester can be gauged for various periods between 1585 and 1702. The population was the same at both dates but movement into the town diminished the effect of higher mortality 1597–1606; it converted a natural loss into a net gain 1637–9. Out-migration turned a birth surplus into a net loss 1616–18 (Alldridge, 1986, *130*). The age and sex structure of migration also influenced marriage chances: if nubile women were over-represented their marriage would be delayed at their new abode –as in seventeenth century London (Clark and Souden, 1987, *23*). However, across England as a whole, Kussmaul finds the net effect of selective migration on nuptiality was weak (1990, *158–63*).

Mobility could therefore contribute to regional demographic differences and thus to national structures and trends. However, there was no effect on total numbers until movers left the country altogether. Permanent migration overseas certainly existed in the sixteenth century and before but the volume of emigration increased significantly in the seventeenth century. Scots were engaged in overseas trade, notably with the Netherlands, the Baltic and the north-west Atlantic coast from the medieval period and can be found as soldiers, farmers, petty merchants and 'professionals' in eastern Europe in the sixteenth and seventeenth centuries. For the middle classes, contacts with European universities were extensive, notably Leiden for law in the seventeenth century. Movement of Scots to the New World was comparatively unimportant before the second half of the eighteenth century. Something like 6,000 left for that destination before 1700, some voluntarily as religious refugees during the 1640s and 1690s, others transported by Oliver Cromwell in the 1650s or by Charles II in the 1670s and 1680s. Convict transportations were increasing from the late seventeenth century but only a few hundred left 1718–75 (Ekirch, 1987, *23–7*). As early as 1740 groups of families began to leave the western isles for the Americas, often led by lesser gentry (Houston and Withers, 1990).

Such numbers are dwarfed by the volume of movement to (and from) Ireland in the seventeenth century. The initial settlement of Ulster involved some 14,000 Scots before 1625 (Flinn, 1977, *8*). In the 1650s, 24,000 Scots went there, and a total of perhaps 100,000 Scots during the seventeenth century. Some 130,000 people left Scotland for north America and Ireland during the seventeenth century. Movement of Scots to England is harder to quantify except for specific groups: the 1,600 men who loaded coal onto the ships bound for London from Newcastle ('keelmen') were almost all Scots-born in the seventeenth century; in the late seventeenth century Scots were prominent in itinerant trading and in London hairdressing and tailoring.

In contrast with the nineteenth century, early modern Ireland was almost certainly a net receiver of people from Scotland and, to a lesser extent, England. One estimate has over a quarter of Ireland's people 'of Scottish and English blood' in 1733. Almost all the Irish Quakers of the seventeenth century were of English extraction. Ulster people moved back to Scotland in periods of political and religious upset during the seventeenth century and at times of severe famine such as the 1620s. There is also evidence of emigration to north America of small farmers and craftsmen from Ulster in the 1720s, 1740s and 1750s (Clarkson, 1988, *231*). Ireland was attractive to Scots because they had more capital and better agricultural techniques than natives, and because political restrictions kept catholics from the land. Taking into account differing perceptions of acceptable living standards, these reasons may explain why Scots moved to Ireland and Irish to Europe and America (Macafee and Morgan, 1981). Military defeats in 1603, 1652 and 1691 prompted an exodus not only of individual Irish officers and soldiers to Europe but also of whole companies or regiments. Irish were a major component of white emigration to the West Indies from the mid seventeenth century and Ulster Scots of movement to north America before 1760. The volume of migration into Ireland was much lower in the early eighteenth century than in the seventeenth. The same is true of emigration from Ireland where one rough estimate is 1–2 per 1,000 in the seventeenth century, 1 per 1,000 in the eighteenth.

Needless to say, English net migration estimates are both more precise and more robust. The figures in Wrigley and Schofield showed migration moving in cycles and peaking in the 1650s. Recent work by Oeppen (1991) has flattened out these 'waves' and presented a more reliable set of estimates. Net emigration was at its highest in the mid sixteenth century and declined almost without interruption until the beginning of the nineteenth century. At 1.7 per 1,000, the net migration rate was higher in the 1560s than at any time between 1541 and 1866. Net migration exerted a powerful influence on population growth during the century *c.* 1650–*c.* 1750 when intrinsic growth rates were low. England's population fell by 385,000 1656–86 and migration accounted for a substantial proportion of this, also slowing early eighteenth century growth significantly (Wrigley and Schofield, 1981, *228*; Oeppen, 1991). At other periods the net loss was lower and the effect on growth rates attenuated. Movement abroad did not merely effect total population. Most English emigrants to the New World were young adults who would have married and reproduced in the colonies. Their movement therefore reduced total fertility among the remaining population. In addition, since most English emigrants were single men their departure may have slightly reduced marriage chances for resident women and thus further limited population growth. Military emigration from seventeenth century Scotland may also be related to the relatively late age at first marriage for women.

Recent work has sought to revise upwards numbers of emigrants. However, in discussing migration estimates, we must be careful to distinguish figures of net from gross emigration or immigration, and those which cover specific groups or destinations from total estimates. Net migration is the total movement out of a country less the numbers who enter it. Between 1630 and 1699, for example, a net total of some 544,000 people left England, 70 per cent of them destined for the New World. Back projection calculations give this figure, including estimates of deaths at sea and by soldiers and traders abroad, but do not show the absolute numbers entering or leaving. Other sources can help here. Indentured servants were young women and men (in a ratio of 1:4 1650–1780) who, like apprentices, agreed to work for a master during a fixed period in return for a paid passage, their keep while serving and certain rights on completion of the indenture (Galenson, 1981). Between 300,000 and 400,000 of these young adults (nearly three-quarters were aged 15–24) left for British colonies 1650–1780, making up perhaps a half to three-quarters of all white settlers of the American colonies. A further quarter of Britons moving to the New World 1718–75 were forcibly transported convicts – made up of approximately 36,000 English, 13,000 Irish and 700 Scots – with an age and sex composition similar to that of free servants (Ekirch, 1987, *23–7, 116*). Most went to the Chesapeake.

There may have been a substantial outflow to the New World colonies compensated for by movement from other parts of Britain or by protestant refugees from Europe. England probably received more Scots people, and possibly also Welsh, than it gave to these regions whereas Ireland was a net recipient of migrants: the commentator Reynel estimated in 1674 that 200,000 people had been 'wasted in repeopling Ireland' (Wrigley and Schofield, 1981, *224*). Knowing the numbers who arrived in the colonies does not show how many stayed there because individuals and families sometimes returned to England, especially in the seventeenth century (Cressy, 1987).

Most migration was voluntary and drawn from a broad spectrum of society: labourers to lairds. However, recent work has shown how complex were the motivations of emigrants. Even the supposedly 'religious' movers to New England in the first half of the seventeenth century had important family and economic reasons for leaving their homeland and Cressy concludes that 'the movement to New England appears untidy, fractured and complex rather than rational, purposeful and coherent' (1987, *74*). To a degree, emigrants may have been responding to specific changes in the economic climate at home but there is no evidence that they were driven out by an acute pressure of population on resources. Desire for betterment rather than mere subsistence characterises most movement. For example, the settler population of early seventeenth century Munster mostly comprised skilled artisans and farmers (Canny, 1985, *13*). English emigrants to the north American colonies were more literate than their counterparts left behind, suggesting above-average status. Criminals were dispatched to the Americas and there was some settlement by soldiers, in parts of Ulster for example, but emigrants were definitely not the dregs of society. As Sir George Peckham remarked in 1583, people emigrated 'in hope thereby to amend their estates' (Galenson, 1981, *112–13*).

Inferring motivation is difficult. However, both the timing of emigration and the composition of migrant groups suggest that narrowing opportunities to improve, or at least maintain, individual or family fortunes at home rather than absolute want were the principal incentives. Furthermore, the overall volume of emigration from Scotland and England grew in the first half of the nineteenth century at a time of economic expansion rather than contraction and stagnation. Those who emigrated seem to have responded positively to better opportunities perceived in new lands. It is true that movement of Scots to Ireland in the 1690s was caused mainly by adverse economic conditions in Scotland and that in the 1770s Scots were more likely to leave Britain for negative reasons – such as landlord exploitation – than were English emigrants. However, emigration should be seen as a positive response more than as a sign of desperation. The *effect* of emigration may have been to improve the balance between population and resources for those remaining but this was probably not the *cause* except in the short term. Migration was a way of preventing any imbalance becoming too serious rather than a simple reaction to over-population. Other means of achieving an equilibrium are discussed in the following chapter.

6
Population, economy and society

Up to this point, we have dealt mainly with the purely demographic components of population structures and trends. Human beings did not, of course, marry, procreate and die in a vacuum. The decisions which they made as individuals or as a society could both reflect and effect their environment. Migration is an example. During the early modern period, their understanding of, and control over, that environment was much weaker than for many modern populations. However, they were by no means wholly victims of circumstances.

In any population, human or animal, there must at some point exist a balance between the demand for food and the ability of an environment to provide it. Several early modern commentators, of course, recognised this, but none developed the idea as clearly as Thomas Malthus. In his *Essay on the Principle of Population*, first printed in 1798 and in subsequent editions, Malthus posited that while food production could only increase arithmetically, population could show compound or geometrical growth. Over time, population growth rates would therefore exceed the rate of increase in agricultural output and living standards would be likely to fall. One way in which population and resources could be brought back into balance was by progressive immiseration, starvation and disease: what Malthus called a 'positive' check. Much more likely was that people, realising their living standards were threatened, would adopt some means of checking population growth before the ravages of high mortality were felt. Malthus called this a 'preventive' check and saw a reduction in nuptiality as the mechanism which would eventually bring population back into line with food supply (Schofield, 1983).

Where do England, Scotland and Ireland fit into this scheme? A demographic regime is an internally coherent population system defined in social and economic terms as well as simply demographic ones. In order fully to understand its functioning and to explain changes in the relative significance of its components we must look beyond purely demographic factors. Economic, social, cultural, legal and ideological considerations may come into play. Throughout, the difference between short- and long-term effects, between simultaneous and lagged ones, and between the relative strengths of relationships is important (Schofield, 1985a, *578–9*).

Mortality

Historians traditionally fell into two camps when it came to explaining population growth rates. In the 1970s the orthodox view was that population and resources would be kept in a sort of balance by periodic outbreaks of famine, war and disease. Some of these would be the direct result of over-population, others accidental. Nuptiality and fertility were felt to be much too slow to respond in the short term to changes in scarcity and plenty, and could not vary enough to make the necessary adjustments (Flinn, 1977). This turned out to be a dangerous assumption to make on both theoretical and empirical grounds. Opposing this view were authorities such as Connell, Habakkuk and Krause who focused on the preventive check which was seen to work through nuptiality and fertility. Changes in nuptiality can indeed have a rapid and pronounced effect on fertility which, for England at least, varied more than mortality over long periods. Wrigley (1981) has shown that three-quarters of the increase in population growth in England in the second half of the eighteenth century can be attributed to rising fertility consequent on a substantial fall in the age at first marriage for women. Studies of the eighteenth century have dominated discussion of the role of nuptiality and fertility in demographic change. However, mortality was of great importance, accounting equally with fertility for changing rates of population growth in England between 1551 and 1751. There are two main issues. First, could people, as individuals or as a society, influence their own life chances at all, and, if so, by what means? Second, was mortality an integral component of the demographic and economic system, linked positively or negatively to other variables such as food supplies and nuptiality?

At first sight, mortality may seem largely exogenous, or linked only weakly, to economic change. This is particularly true of England. Just 16 per cent of short-run mortality variation from the sixteenth to the early nineteenth century was associated with price changes and the long-term relationship was 'disorderly and frequently contrary to expectation' (Schofield, 1983, 276–7, 282). In England, mortality did respond to short-term monthly and annual changes in food prices up to 1640. During the following century the relationship weakened then disappeared altogether (Wrigley and Schofield, 1981, 285–355, 368–77, 412–17). Galloway has shown for England 1675–1755 that just a quarter of fluctuations in deaths of those over age five were associated with fluctuations in grain prices (compared with nearly a half in France) and that the magnitude of the mortality increase in the year of harvest failure and in the following year was only half that of France (1985). Long-run trends in scarcity and plenty shown by wage rates were not related to mortality in early modern England.

England conquered the problem of famine at an early stage in her development. What is more, recent work suggests that the importance of famine in the late sixteenth and early seventeenth century has been overestimated and defences against it underrated. Even in years of serious shortage such as 1597–8 when mortality was 26 per cent over its long-term trend, only 28 per cent of parishes in the Cambridge Group sample suffered from subsistence crises (Walter, 1989, 79). Walter identifies vulnerability to famine increased by 'the weakness of local ecologies, fragile surpluses, poor and unfavourable market integration' and economic specialisation (81) while 'the more mixed the economy the greater were the defences against harvest failure' (92). The last serious famines in the 1620s seem mainly to have affected certain northern pastoral areas. Indeed, Walter cautions against exaggerating vulnerability to famine in England because of extensive formal and informal support mechanisms (1989, 92–116). English agriculture expanded sufficiently between the late fifteenth and early nineteenth century to cope with a fourfold increase in population. By the end of the seventeenth century wheat prices moved in unison, demonstrating that a national market existed for that grain (though not others) (Walter and Schofield, 1989, *9–10*). English poor relief, codified in laws of 1597 and 1601, was based on compulsory rating of better-off parishioners and was very effective nationally by the 1630s.

This does not necessarily mean that nobody starved. 'Hidden hunger' may still have haunted sections of the population. In communities with extreme wealth polarisation, such as the cloth areas of Essex during the 1629 trade slump, poor-law rating alone could not cope. Nor does it mean that agricultural productivity was always sufficiently elastic to meet the needs of a growing population. In periods when population grew at more than 0.5 per cent a year the greater proportional fall in real wages suggests otherwise. If population grew at more than 1 per cent a year then food prices would rise at 1.5 per cent per annum – as in the late sixteenth century (Wrigley and Schofield, 1981, *404*). The most fertile period for the dissemination of agricultural improvements in England came between 1660 and 1740. They were stimulated by falling profitability and changing demand structures rather than by the pressure of population – which was in fact much weaker than a century before (Kussmaul, 1991). Agricultural change came about more in response to changing population composition – more urban and rural non-agricultural workers – than to growth itself.

In Scotland and Ireland, low agricultural productivity, restricted marketing and inadequate poor relief undoubtedly contributed to continued vulnerability to famine, notably in Scotland in the 1690s and in Ireland in the 1720s and 1740s (Dickson, 1988; Post, 1985). In some Scottish towns recorded burials during the dearth years 1623–4 were up to eight times as high as surrounding years (Flinn, 1977, *6–7*). However, it is difficult to argue that a Malthusian 'positive check' was truly an integral part of Scotland's demographic and economic system. Crises like the 1690s may have helped alleviate any population pressure but the unexpected nature of the famine of 1695–9 is shown by the passing of an act by the Scottish parliament in early 1695 to subsidise grain exports at a time of low prices (Flinn, 1977, *165*). Ireland too was a net exporter of grain in the 1700s and 1710s though there were heavy imports in the second quarter of the eighteenth century (Clarkson, 1988, *223*; Dickson, 1988, *101*). By the early eighteenth century there was no close connection between grain prices and mortality in Scotland (Flinn, 1977, *211*).

In both Scotland and Ireland, poor relief was permissive rather than obligatory, based on voluntary donations and landowners' charity. For most of the period before 1750, Scottish landowners steadfastly refused to be rated. Some East Lothian parishes did have effective poor relief in the 1690s and this protected them from the worst effects of famine mortality but it was not until well into the eighteenth century that provisions worked efficiently over large areas of Scotland. The shortages of 1740–1 were dealt with much more effectively than those of the 1690s by supplying grain to markets, providing substantial voluntary relief and creating employment.

Irish poor relief in the early eighteenth century was essentially private and local, based on the charity of landlords, clergy and neighbourly 'generosity of the have-littles towards the have-nots' (Dickson, 1988, *105–6*). The parish was a unit of government and administration never really took root in Ireland because of the late development of the established (but minority) church of Ireland as an effective ecclesiastical organisation. New means of relief were being tried in Ulster in the late 1720s though their effect was limited. In parts of Ireland, absence of a resident landlord may have prevented employment projects and sales of subsidised grain being implemented (Flinn, 1977, *7, 13*; Post, 1985, *146–7, 176–7*). Problems were exacerbated because in Ireland doctrinal divisions followed those of wealth and poverty: catholics were usually poorer than protestants. This illustrates the point that hunger is not solely related to harvest shortages but is tied to a range of other entitlements which may worsen or ease its burden. The fact that Ireland escaped lightly from the European famines of the 1690s and relatively lightly in 1708–10 may also show that an element of meterological luck was involved.

Most subsistence crises were not a structural part of the demographic and economic regime but were accidental. Admittedly, in Scotland the problems of sort-term grain shortage were exacerbated by chronically low net grain yields, limited transport and marketing mechanisms, and a relatively ineffective poor-relief system before the eighteenth century. The example of Shetland suggests that people could cope with one dearth year, even if it involved bad harvests, shortage of fish and cattle disease (1663), but that runs of bad years like 1633–5 or 1693–6 in these islands elicited statements about widespread deaths from starvation (Flinn, 1977, *114, 130*). Admittedly too, Scotland was not 'a region of a larger international economy' as was the Netherlands. This had important implications for the overall standard of living and for the existence for some brief periods of a negative relationship between food prices and population size since the demographic/economic system was more likely to be closed (De Vries, 1985, *679–81*). Again, the problems of securing grain from external sources improved in the eighteenth century. Yet, there is little point in piling up examples of local subsistence crises since this does not allow systematic measurement of the strength or consistency of the relationship between prices and mortality. Recent work by Gibson and Smout (1992) has given an outline of wages and prices in some areas of Scotland, but without firm evidence on changing levels of underlying mortality there is no way of proving a long-term connection between the variables.

Harvest failures had wide-ranging effects in societies where a half or more of household expenditure went on food stuffs (Walter, 1989, *81–6*). Having access to grain markets might be of little help if people had no money to buy. Communities specialising in pastoral agricultural products or in industrial production may have been unable to sell their products to those spending their all on grain. Cumbria in the 1620s was particularly vulnerable. There were social as well as economic implications, one noted by the Scotsman David Calderwood during the autumn of 1621: 'Every man was careful to ease himself of such persons as he might spare, and to live as retiredly as possibly he might. Pitiful was the lamentation not only of vaging [wandering] beggars, but also of honest persons' (Flinn, 1977, *122*). The closer a farmer was to subsistence under a regime of low net yields, the less likely he would be to have a surplus which could be used to feed employees or to sell. If he had to go into the market during a dearth to buy food for workers whose contracts included diet, the effect could be disastrous. Furthermore, in societies where a half of family expenditure went on grain-based foods, changes in grain prices would have a disproportionate effect on income for non-food purchases and demand for non-agricultural goods and services (Wrigley, 1989).

The comment about wandering beggars also reminds us that higher mortality in years of shortage may have been partly due to disease. Social as well as biological links may have existed between dearth and death (Walter and Schofield, 1989, *18–20, 53–4*). From one angle, economic diversification and good welfare provisions might not protect a population against a surge in mortality associated with social upheaval: England in 1742 is a clear example (Post, 1985, *93, 279*). Better urban than rural poor relief in Scotland and Ireland encouraged an influx of beggars: between 1740 and 1741 a mortality index for rural Munster rose 53 per cent, for urban Munster 90 per cent (Post, 1985, *152, 245*). In that sense, good poor relief could have an adverse effect on a community's overall mortality. Public policy which reduced unemployment, migration, vagrancy and begging had the best chance of minimising the risk of epidemic disease.

Poor-relief provisions would help to alleviate starvation but could do little to prevent disease mortality unless they encouraged the poor to remain in their parishes. Medical intervention was largely ineffective in dealing with morbid diseases at this time, with the possible exception of inoculation which was being tried out in the 1740s and 1750s (Porter, 1987). Once a person was infected there was little chance effectively to change the disease's course. Other biological links have recently been questioned, notably the commonly posited relationship between malnutrition and disease morbidity. A link between malnutrition and higher case fatality for tuberculosis, diarrhoea, measles and some respiratory infections exists. The biological effect of poor nutrition on the chances of contracting, or dying from, other diseases is highly questionable (Post, 1985, *273*). Plague, smallpox, malaria and typhoid were so virulent that chances of survival had little to do with nutrition. The short-term link between prices and fertility in England was less through amenorrhoea resulting from malnutrition than through foetal loss during pregnancy (Wrigley and Schofield, 1981, *363–6, 368–73*). Finally, similarities between the mortality of a privileged group such as peers and ordinary English people before 1750 support the notion that nutrition and medical care can have played little part in explaining life expectancy.

Looked at in another way, the relationship may seem paradoxical. Economic 'progress' rather than backwardness may have increased mortality since the development of overseas trade, urban growth and the integration of domestic markets may have accelerated the distribution of disease pathogens by increasing the volume of contacts between carriers and potential victims. If part of England was vulnerable to subsistence crises, the more densely settled south-east was prone to disease epidemics, a pattern which seems to have persisted until the 1720s (Schofield, 1983, *287*; Dobson, 1989b). Rising real income may increase mortality by drawing more people into towns to fulfil demand for goods and services (Wrigley and Schofield, 1981, *415*). In Scotland, the proliferation of market centres in the second half of the seventeenth century, coupled with comparatively rapid urbanisation 1650–1750, may help to account for the shift from epidemic to endemic smallpox and other diseases. We might speculate that seasonal migration from Highlands to Lowlands from the later seventeenth century may have exposed more Highlanders to the endemic smallpox of the Lowlands, thus integrating disease pools and raising mortality in Highland areas contributing to the flows.

A further paradox hinted at above is that economic specialisation may have increased vulnerability to famine. Growing dependence on a particular food could have this effect. For example, potatoes were an important but not yet staple food in parts of late seventeenth century Ireland. Described, by the commentator Madden in the 1730s, as a substitute food for a quarter of the year, potatoes took hold in Munster and were the main winter diet of the cottier and lesser tenant classes in many parts of Ireland by the 1690s and perhaps earlier – except in Ulster where porridge and root vegetables were preferred. Failure of both cereal crops and potatoes during 1740–1 certainly contributed to the severity of famine in south-west Ireland (Post, 1985, *97*). The potato was of less importance in Scotland before the mid eighteenth century.

Growing dependence on a particular type of production could have a similar effect. Areas of Scotland which specialised in pastoral husbandry might be particularly unfortunate. Most Hebridean islands grew grain for subsistence but those such as Mull which concentrated on cattle-raising suffered badly from the 1690s' dearths. After 1700 Highlanders were exposed to the adverse effects of uncertain markets which allowed them to sell cattle and buy grain (Walter and Schofield, 1989, *33*). If demand for livestock fell, those in specialist cattle-raising regions would have less money to buy grain. People could make choices about work and lifestyle but it was not always possible to control the demographic outcomes of these decisions.

The potential for human action can be illustrated by efforts to prevent plague. The reasons behind the disappearance of plague from Britain during the seventeenth century are the subject of considerable debate (Slack, 1985). Some argue that human beings had little control over plague and that changes in the disease itself or in the rat population which carried it must explain its demise. Mortality from disease is a function of three things: exposure to infection, levels of resistance and the frequency and virulence of different strains of pathogen (Landers, 1990, *30*). However, in the case of plague we have to understand the four main stages in its spread in order to judge the role of different agencies in banishing its scourge. The transmission of the most common form of plague, bubonic, depends on the existence of a pool of resistant rats and fleas who can carry the disease without dying of it. Plague epidemics of the sixteenth and seventeenth centuries seem to have been the result of periodic reintroductions from abroad – possibly from the Netherlands which had worldwide trade connections. At this point, humans could prevent the transmission of plague by quarantine measures. Once introduced into Britain, plague spread from town to town at a pace which suggests that humans rather than rats transmitted the disease, or perhaps rats on baggage and bulk food carts. At this second stage too, people could throw up sanitary cordons to prevent the entry of infected persons into their communities (Slack, 1985).

The coherent suite of policies – at household, local and national level – which had developed to counter plague by the middle of the seventeenth century focused on the actions of people. The importance of rats was not understood until the end of the nineteenth century. This meant that if steps were taken early on, plague deaths could be prevented, but that efforts to curb an epidemic in its two latter stages would be much less successful. Once introduced into a community, plague took root in suburbs and back alleys away from main centres of intercourse, pointing to rats as the bearers of disease. At the level of the household, the lack of correlation between mortality and household size, and the way plague left some houses unaffected, suggests that the frequency of human contact was much less significant than the numbers and movements of rodents carrying infection. For this reason, attempts to quarantine infected households were likely to prove unsuccessful once plague had a grip. There was, admittedly, an element of chance in all this: restrictions on movement prevented serious mortality at Exeter in 1665–6 but not at Norwich, at Linlithgow but not at Leith in the 1640s (Slack, 1985; Flinn, 1977, *137*).

As noted above, levels of mortality from disease depend in part on the extent of human exposure and resistance to infections. Diseases which killed readily in one period may be much less deadly in another or many disappear altogether from a country over time. Riley has recently claimed that the eighteenth century mortality decline was the result of fewer and less severe epidemics because 'a medicine of avoidance and prevention' developed to reduce human contact with disease (1987). Biological hypotheses about disease morbidity and mortality changes are extremely difficult to test: Riley's fails to document changing deaths by cause and by transmission vector or to assess the value of medical advice and intervention. Reductions in mortality may be attributable to changes in human action but they may also be the result of factors over which men and women had no control. Changes in diseases and immunological adjustments by humans may have taken place, though while the adjustment may have been 'mutual', changes in microbe genetics occur much more rapidly than among human. Before *c.* 1750 the modest rate and scale of changing mortality is consistent with this explanation (among others), but probably not after that date.

The role of resistance is clearly illustrated in the age structure of mortality in late seventeenth and early eighteenth century London. Adult life expectancy above age 30 differed little between London Quakers and anglicans living in rural parishes and small market towns. However, infant, child and young adult mortality was much higher in the metropolis. Among south London Quakers all those aged 10 years or older who died from smallpox were immigrants to the city. Native-born adults had high levels of immunity but incomers did not. Much excess urban mortality was occasioned by 'the action of density dependent immunising infections' (Landers, 1990, *52, 54, 59*).

Not all diseases confer immunity. Some gastric and respiratory fevers could be 'debilitating, recurrent and progressive' (Dobson, 1989b, *418–19*). Commenting on the increase in background mortality across south-east England *c.* 1640–1720, Dobson writes of 'an epidemiological crisis fuelled by pathogens and peoples moving across the countryside and oceans' (1989b, *421*). For example, malaria may have been brought into south-east England by Dutch settlers in the sixteenth century. Diseases nurtured in south-east England went with emigrants to the New World. New diseases being introduced between the mid sixteenth and the mid seventeenth centuries would affect children above the age of weaning and this would explain the marked worsening of mortality among those aged 1–9 years compared with that of infants (Schofield and Wrigley, 1979, *67–9*). Children fed at the breast are much less likely to become infected by water- and food-borne gastric diseases than those fed artificially. In addition, human breast milk contains antibodies which confer a degree of immunity on the suckling infant. English infants whose mother died soon after birth, and who were deprived of breast milk, were three times as likely to die by age one than the general infant mortality rate (Wrigley and Schofield, 1983, *183*).

Finally, wholly exogenous factors such as weather also played a role. A fall of 1° C in summer temperature reduced annual mortality by 4 per cent (Wrigley and Schofield, 1981, *384–98*). Endemic respiratory infections or typhus increased as a result of lower winter temperatures while higher summer ones facilitated the diffusion of bacteria causing dysentery and typhoid. The late seventeenth century 'ice age' created these conditions.

In conclusion, mortality was only partly endogenous to the economic and demographic regime. For England it is clear that mortality was not 'regularly and substantially affected by changes in living standards' (Wrigley and Schofield, 1981, *354*). It does not seem to have acted as an equilibriating mechanism. In some areas, such as agricultural improvements and poor relief, people acted with varying degrees of success to prevent excessive strain on resources being corrected by mortality. For Scotland and perhaps Ireland, abrupt short-term adjustments through mortality may have occurred in times of famine – as occasionally happened in England. It is unclear whether a long-term equilibrium between population and resources was maintained by mortality in Scotland and it almost certainly was not in Ireland. Overall, it seems that mortality was only weakly integrated into the economic system and for most purposes it should be seen as an independent variable.

Nuptiality

North-west European societies of the sixteenth, seventeenth and eighteenth centuries differed fundamentally both from contemporary eastern and southern Europe and from peasant or tribal societies in the modern world. The most important difference lay in the nature of the early modern household and in the preconditions of family formation (Hajnal, 1983; Smith, 1981; 1984). Social and cultural norms dictated that couples wishing to marry and procreate should possess sufficient resources to establish independent households. Those households would normally be economically and physically separate from those of kin. This explains the contrast between the large, sometimes complex households characteristic of eastern and southern Europe – numbering 10–15 souls and often including more than one married couple – and the small, simple nuclear family households found in north-western Europe. It also explains why women waited until they were roughly 23–26 years old before marrying for the first time and why, over the early modern period as a whole, one woman in eight never married. In eastern Europe almost all women were married by age 20. Couples joined existing, large households made up of their kin.

The time between puberty and marriage in Britain and Ireland was filled for the majority by a period working in another household as a servant or apprentice. Servants were typically young, single men and women aged 15–25 who worked in agriculture or, for females, as domestics in return for board and lodging. In the late seventeenth and early eighteenth centuries 18 per cent of England's population were servants: most of the relevant age group (Kussmaul, 1981). Apprentices signed a contract binding them to work for a master for a set period in return for training and keep. Average age at indenture for London apprentices in the late sixteenth and early seventeenth centuries was 18 or 19 years, in seventeenth century Newcastle and Edinburgh approximately 15 or 16 years. Young men served terms of 5–7 years on average, meaning they would be in their early to mid twenties when they started working as journeymen and making their own living. Apprentices were prevented from marrying and the institution checked early marriage. There was no formal restraint on servants marrying. Service was an opportunity for not marrying and for saving to reach the accepted threshold of economic independence necessary to marry.

In early modern Britain, marriage formation was linked to economic opportunity but the precise relationship varied regionally. We noted in Chapter 2 that between 1551 and 1751 fertility and mortality contributed almost equally to changes in England's intrinsic growth rate. However, movements in fertility were twice as large as those in mortality during these two centuries. In Chapter 3 we saw that nuptiality was the main force behind changing fertility. Why should age at first marriage and proportions never married alter? The simple answer is that people married on the expectation of economic independence and continued well-being. Their changing perceptions of economic opportunity provide the key. However, recent research has painted a more complicated picture of nuptiality's context.

Armed with estimates of changing population over time, and of the relative significance of fertility and mortality in those trends, and equipped with an indicator of changing economic opportunity it has already been possible to demonstrate for England the lack of a long-term connection between scarcity and plenty, and mortality. When the same economic indicator is set alongside changes in nuptiality and fertility the association is clear and striking. Over the long term, the curves representing real wages and the gross reproduction rate move in waves separated by 30–40 years. When population rose at more than approximately 0.5 per cent a year, real wages fell. After a period during which English society became aware of the worsening balance between population and resources, levels of nuptiality would fall either by raising age at first marriage for women or by increasing the proportion of women never married, or both. This reduced fertility and brought growth rates down. In times of plenty when growth rates were less than 0.5 per cent, nuptiality would also adjust to improved economic opportunities and the cycle would begin again (Wrigley and Schofield, 1981, *402–14, 466–80*). Flinn contends that demographic–economic interactions must be arranged in a linear hierarchy, but within a demographic system relationships can operate in both directions (1982, *455*). This seems to be the case in early modern England for both positive and negative feedbacks existed within the system.

As Malthus suggested, there were long, slow fluctuations in the rate of population growth in England which were associated with the standard of living. While the long-term relationship between nuptiality and price fluctuations is clear, that between the variables in the short term is no less marked. A doubling of grain prices in any one year produced a lasting reduction in the 'normal' number of marriages over a five-year period of more than a fifth (Schofield, 1983, *282*). Rises in mortality associated with disease epidemics had the predictable effect of raising nuptiality in the short-term though this was more through remarriages rather than by creating more openings in the economy for first marriages. The net effect on fertility was slight because a widow remarrying would not necessarily have had any more children than if her husband had remained alive.

Wrigley and Schofield's interpretation of population-resource links is surprisingly traditional and lacking in statistical sophistication compared with their analysis of purely demographic relationships – perhaps because theories which link population to resources are still rudimentary. For example, is the long time-lag believable; what components of nuptiality were affected by changing real wages; and did changes in the social and occupational composition of the population influence the relationship? Weir ((1984) and modified by Schofield (1985b)) has addressed these questions, arguing that a change in the economic climate affected only a part of the population and, until the eighteenth century, had most influence on the chances of ever marrying rather than on age at marriage. The main effect of a growth in real wages was a reduction in celibacy. Marriage depended on economic independence gained either by the transmission of property from older to younger generation or through the pooling of labour resources of husband and wife. When times were hard, fewer people could surmount this threshold and may have been denied the chance to marry. Differential effects may have existed. For example, adverse economic circumstances may reduce marriage chances but if conditions affect female employment opportunities particularly badly they may be encouraged to marry because of the difficulties of subsisting as single women. Economic differences between regions may have exaggerated or reduced such changes. In pastoral areas with more regular employment for women the effects of an economic downturn may have been attenuated.

Studies of socially specific trends in nuptiality are rare for the early modern period. One, of Colyton in Devon, demonstrates two important points. First, male and female marriage ages did not move in tandem. Second, trends in age at first marriage for women from labouring backgrounds were very different from those of gentry or the poor 1550–1750. For the period 1538–1799 an almost identical proportion of gentry, crafts and labouring women never married by age 45 (just over 5 per cent) but nearly 13 per cent of women who were poor or who came from impoverished families never began reproductive careers (Sharpe, 1991).

Goldstone (1986) reinforces and refines the contention that until the middle of the eighteenth century changes in nuptiality were mainly caused by rises or falls in the proportions of women ever married rather than by changes in age at first marriage. For the period up to *c.* 1750 he identifies two types of marriers. First, 'traditional' marriers covering a wide range of ages whose behaviour changed relatively little over time because they were always above the threshold of economic independence – probably because they relied on transfers of wealth before parental death or on the inheritance of property. Second, 'non-marriers' whose proportion of the population changed significantly over time. Among the cohort born 1604–28 22 per cent never married by age 45 compared with 12 per cent for 1704–28 (Goldstone, 1986, *17*). Marriage chances for this group were determined by the opportunity for personal saving, itself primarily related to changes in real income. Those close to the conventional threshold of economic independence were most vulnerable to changing economic circumstances. Goldstone argues that 'for the cohorts born before 1700 swings in the proportion ever married clearly were large, independent of changes in the age at first marriage, and dominated the movement of fertility' (1986, *10*). For example, a 50 per cent increase in real wages between the early seventeenth and early eighteenth centuries had almost no effect on age at first marriage for both sexes. Whether the shift to age at marriage as the main determinant of changing fertility in the middle of the eighteenth century constitutes a 'revolution' is more debateable since the responsiveness of nuptiality *as a whole* to real wage trends remained similar over long periods.

Goldstone has made a further contribution by using a more geographically extensive and complete series of agricultural and industrial prices as a proxy for real wages. Measuring the economic environment in a pre-statistical age is notoriously difficult and historians have to use a range of more or less reliable indicators. Best known of these is the Phelps Brown and Hopkins index of wages and prices. This suffers from long periods of missing data, especially in the first half of the seventeenth century. Goldstone's alternative series fills this gap and shows that real wages did not begin to rise until the 1650s while the gross reproduction rate rose from the 1670s. A lag of 15–20 years between changes in real wages and population is more believable than Wrigley and Schofield's 30–40 years because it would take ordinary people a decade or two to accumulate savings as servants or apprentices and then during a period of working independently as labourers or journeymen (Goldstone, 1986, *7–8, 15*).

It is fortunate that Goldstone and others have reworked the Phelps Brown and Hopkins index, for it has been heavily criticised. Wrigley and Schofield acknowledge that 'the statistical base of the real-wages index is partial, limited and fragile' (1981, *354, 407–8, 411–12*). Others have reworked and updated the wage and prices indices, leaving the trends intact but adjusting the level and fine-tuning the timing of changes in direction. By substituting retail for wholesale prices as the basis of his index, Rappaport has shown that during the sixteenth century in London real wages declined only half as much as Phelps Brown and Hopkins believed. Shortcomings in the real wage series are most apparent in the long run since they do not fully reflect changes in consumption pattern or the amount of work available, especially for women and children whose contribution to the total family budget was often considerable but whose work opportunities were much more volatile in the long-term than those of adult males (Snell, 1985; Rappaport,

1989). However, if changing demand for female and child labour worked in the same direction as that for adult males the resulting fluctuations in family income would have been more extreme. It should be stressed that, in spite of revisions to the wage and price series, and in spite of debates over the time-lag between changing real wages and population growth rates, the long-term relationship between the variables in England is very striking and of great importance.

The population–resource equation is complicated for England by the presence of institutional factors which could influence demographic behaviour. An unusual feature of England in the seventeenth and eighteenth centuries was the blending of economic individualism with social and political collectivism. Economic and residential independence at marriage existed along-side a compulsory community welfare system which supported families at points when there were too many dependent mouths to feed (Smith, 1981). By contrast, the poor-relief system in Scotland may have discouraged early marriage because poorer couples perceived that surplus resources in the society were scanty and that they would have to shoulder the potential burden of poverty by themselves, or with informal help from equally impoverished neighbours or kin. In Ireland, abundance of resources compensated for lack of an effective poor-relief scheme under most economic conditions.

Finding the resources to create a new household depends, in an agrarian society, on access to land. The most obvious mechanism linking population and resources would be deaths in the older generation releasing property for sons to marry. Improving life expectancy in eighteenth century France was associated with reduced nuptiality because there were fewer 'dead men's shoes' to fill (Schofield, 1989, 299). For this reason, the laws and customs relating to inheritance of property have been seen as important determinants of household structure and demographic behaviour. 'Impartible' inheritance, where land passes intact to one person (usually the eldest son), may restrict the number of new households, while delaying marriages and encouraging migration among other children. Partible inheritance divides land and may have had the reverse effect. The role of partible and impartible inheritance has been hotly debated but it was less important in Britain than elsewhere in Europe and nowhere should it be viewed deterministically (Smith, 1984). In Scotland most land was owned by a relatively small number of landowners and worked by tenant farmers, with their live-in single servants, and cottagers who received use rights in exchange for family labour on the main farm. Continuity of tenure was possible and owner-occupation was increasing during the sixteenth and late seventeenth century but the main factors determining availability of land were landlord policy and the market in leasehold farms. Cottars who, with their families, made up the majority of the Lowland population, were wholly dependent on tenant farmers (Houston and Whyte, 1989, *3–20*).

In Ireland, the issue was an abundance of land and ample opportunities for the cheap acquisition of farms. Buoyant real wages in Dublin during the seventeenth century reflected the shortage of skilled labour and the generally healthy state of the economy. Under certain circumstances, rapid population growth is not incompatible with a rising standard of living. Conceivably, Irish labour productivity grew sufficiently in the seventeenth and early eighteenth centuries to cope with population increase (Dickson *et al.*, 1982, *175*). Most agricultural labourers were married and had their own plots of land. There were large numbers of single female servants with a median age in the mid-20s in listings from county Dublin and Munster in the 1650s (Dickson, 1990). However, with age at first marriage for women in the low 20s, it seems that the constraint placed on nuptiality by a decade of service between puberty and marriage was less important in Ireland than in England or Lowland Scotland.

Landholding systems were more complex in England and there were many more small owner-occupiers, at least before the later seventeenth century. Recent research has shown that even where impartible inheritance was practised, parents made every effort to provide as generously for other children (both while still alive and in their wills) as for the one inheriting land (Wrightson, 1982). Given the ease of contracting marriage, and the weak parental or communal control over household formation for most people, inheritance cannot have been an important factor in adjusting population to resources. England's economy contained a large wage-labour component from the sixteenth century, if not before, and most land changed hands by purchase or sale rather than by inheritance from kin. Perhaps a third of England's population in the seventeenth century depended on wage-labour and could therefore have little expectation of inheriting property. At the same time, roughly two-fifths of fathers would have had no surviving sons at their death and a further fifth would have had no children at all to succeed them; some, of course, would have had more than one son (Schofield, 1976, *153*). This means that niches would be created within the economic system but that they would be filled by marriage or purchase rather than by inheritance. For some groups such as copyholders (a form of manorial land tenure), marriage may have been linked to property inheritance. But for much of English society, demographic, and possibly economic, events in the household from which marriers came may have had little direct effect on the formation of a new family (Smith, 1981, *602*).

The prevalence of wage-labour and growing non-agricultural employment opportunities highlights the importance of the wider economy. England and Scotland slowly became more urbanised 1500–1750 and in addition more rural dwellers worked in some form of industry such as mining or textiles. By 1750 a sixth of England's population lived in large towns and a further quarter were rural industrial workers. In other words, more niches were available for those wishing to marry and establish new households outside a purely agrarian context. Some historians have argued that the expansion of these industrial employments could short-circuit the usual wait for inheritance or the time spent between puberty and marriage working as a servant in husbandry or as a domestic servant in one of the growing towns (Levine, 1977). Expanding domestic and overseas demand fostered an increase in textile output not from factories but by increasing the number of traditional family production units. Because start-up costs were low and specialist skills were not needed, couples could marry at an early age. Some have sought the reasons for accelerating population growth in Ireland after the middle of the eighteenth century in the effect of rural industry on nuptiality (Dickson *et al.*, 1982, *173–4*).

In reality, the picture is much more complicated. Rural domestic industry, sometimes called 'proto-industry', certainly expanded in parts of Britain and Ireland: in the west country, midlands and north of England, especially between 1660 and 1740. Total nuptiality was greater in rural industrial parishes (and in market towns) than in agricultural communities. However, it has proved impossible conclusively to link the economic makeup of a parish with age at first marriage for women (Houston and Snell, 1984; Kussmaul, 1990, *141–4*). Nor was rural industry always connected with faster population growth. The 66 parishes in north-east Scotland which had stocking-knitters in 1761 and the 33 where the spinning of linen yarn was widely practised had significantly lower population growth rates over the eighteenth century than the region's small towns. English parishes which had dual industrial and agricultural employments rather than solely industrial ones could maintain a high age at marriage (Kussmaul, 1990, *141–2, 154, 157–8*). Other explanations of any apparent connection between domestic industry and population growth are possible. Entrepreneurs who controlled some forms of rural domestic industry may have chosen to establish ties with parishes which were already growing rapidly because abundant labour supply would keep down costs (Kussmaul, 1990, *139*).

The key to understanding the uneven impact of proto-industrialisation on population trends lies in the context in which proletarianisation took place. If increases in the numbers of wage-dependent workers occurred against a background of rising unemployment, nuptiality would be reduced because more people would not reach the socially acceptable economic threshold for marriage. This was clearly the situation in 1550–1650 when population growth outran employment opportunities. Eighteenth century economic expansion created a much more favourable climate for marriers. However, in England, trends in age at first marriage appear to have followed regional or national economic fortunes rather than strictly local ones. The same may be true of regions of eighteenth century Ireland (Macafee, 1987).

Turning from the specific role of inheritance and rural domestic industry to the general, long-term relationship between population and resources, Scotland's population may not have responded to changing economic circumstances in the same way as England's. No estimates of nuptiality exist for the sixteenth and early seventeenth century. However, the population pressure of the second half of the sixteenth century may have provoked a major change in diet from one with a large meat component to a mainly cereal-based one. What grains were consumed – oats in the form of meal – are generally seen as inferior foods: the English ate wheat bread. With stable agricultural output, a given amount of land could support more mouths under crops than under pasture (Gibson and Smout, 1992). Opportunities to farm new land were strictly limited. Wage and price series for the sixteenth century are scanty but the real wages (expressed as oatmeal purchasing power) of Edinburgh labourers and masons fell sharply c. 1560–c. 1590. Assuming that a dietary change of this nature represents a reduced standard of living, Scottish society may have opted for more people at the expense of quality of life. The shift from a meat-dominated diet to a largely grain-based one during the later sixteenth century may reflect a decision to tolerate a high fertility (or at least a *stable* nuptiality and fertility?) regime and not to make the sort of adjustments elsewhere in the demographic system which happened in early modern England. Purely economic responses to popula-tion growth were probably also inadequate since until the eight-eenth century agricultural productivity remained low, overseas trade small in scale, industrial diversification slight. The situation in England and Scotland, where between roughly 1560 and 1620 the economy failed to expand sufficiently to mop up surplus population, was partly corrected in the 1620s and 1630s in Scot-land but imbalances may have persisted much longer north of the border. As a pure speculation, it may be that the imbalance in Scotland after c. 1560 was caused by autonomous improvements in mortality.

A simultaneous rise in marriage age in the late sixteenth century cannot be ruled out but there is no way of telling. Stability in age at first marriage over long periods does not necessarily prove the absence of a connection between real wage trends and nuptiality. Rural real wages in Scotland were stable 1680–1770 and did not follow the cycles apparent in England. Real wages were increasing in early eighteenth century Glasgow and those of Edinburgh labourers were rising strongly 1740–80, though those of their employers such as masons were easing (Houston, 1988; Gibson and Smout, 1992). The near trebling of proportions urban may indicate growing real incomes 1650–1750: towns provided goods and services on which people could spend their surplus income. But the demand which urban growth reflects may have come from a restricted section of Scottish society: from the rural middling and upper ranks, and from the urban population itself.

The absolute standard of living remained lower in Scotland than England and wealth was more obviously polarised between mercantile, professional and landed classes and the bulk of Scotland's people. Furthermore, the dietary changes of the later sixteenth century were partially reversed in the second half of the eighteenth in prosperous parts of the central Lowlands, lending credence to the idea that adjustments of population and resources were not achieved through nuptiality in Scotland. A high and stable age at first marriage for women over long periods adds weight to this hypothesis. Extensive and possibly unvarying female celibacy over long periods suggests that adjustment was not obtained through this mechanism. In 1782, J. M'Farlan's *Inquiries Concerning the Poor* set out projects to encourage Scotland's poor to marry as a way of fostering population growth and economic change. Late marriage and high celibacy persisted until the second half of the nineteenth century as embedded customs which had outlived the economic circumstances which brought them into being.

The relative inflexibility of marriage ages in Scotland and, probably, Ireland may reflect economic circumstances more than different cultural norms. If Quakers can be taken to represent Ireland's population as a whole, age at first marriage for women rose steadily from the early 20s *c.* 1600 to the late 20s *c.* 1800. This may show 'frontier' conditions giving way to more 'normal' constraints on nuptiality. Scotland may have had less leeway in the economic and demographic system than England or Ireland. Low gross grain yields, of the kind known to characterise Scottish agriculture, involve a high mean annual variation in net yields left for human consumption (Wrigley, 1989, *258–9, 263*; Whyte, 1979). Gibson and Smout show substantial annual and decadal variations in real wages. Sharp variations from year to year in the standard of living will render the population more susceptible to famine and associated diseases. In such an environment, and without extensive non-agricultural employments, the great uncertainties in obtaining the economic independence on which marriage depended might encourage an extremely cautious nuptiality response: women marrying late and a high percentage never at all. Without the cushion of adequate poor relief, couples would be doubly reluctant to marry. This combination, as much as the role of extreme protestantism, may also explain the low levels of pre-nuptial pregnancy obtaining in Scotland before the second half of the eighteenth century. To speculate, Scotland's high celibacy and late age at first marriage for women may be linked to mortality in the same way as France's – as mortality falls, age at marriage and proportions never married will rise – implying a *relatively* high expectation of life at birth given available economic resources.

What all this means is that although England, Scotland and Ireland clearly fit into the north-west European marriage pattern, they did so in distinctive ways. Whatever the imperfections in wage and price series, the link between nuptiality and fertility on the one hand, and economic opportunity on the other, seems firmly established for England. It was not paralleled in Scotland. The method of adjusting population to resources was quite different: changes in diet, migration and (possibly) mortality. For early modern Ireland the balance between population and resources was less of an issue. If there was a response within the system it lay in migration possibly coupled with a gently rising first marriage age for women.

All the above are variations on the 'preventive' check but the role of Malthus' main mechanism, nuptiality, varied. Even in England, the preventive check was only effective over a long time-span: Lee estimates that only a quarter of population growth in one generation would be self-corrected by a real wage response (Wrigley and Schofield, 1989, *xxvii*). Nor was the mechanism always efficient: it tended to 'over-shoot'. Differences in power relations between employers and employees meant that between *c.* 1650 and 1750 when population stagnated and real wages rose, farmers' demand for live-in servants rather than expensive wage labourers held back nuptiality and exerted a 'dysfunctional' check (Schofield, 1989, *303–4*).

The implications for what was perceived to be an acceptable standard of living, and on demand for non-agricultural products, are profound. In Scotland, a low-pressure nuptiality and fertility regime created a lower equilibrium level of population than obtained in Ireland. In that sense, an adjustment had been made

but the balance achieved was precarious and the relative
of living for the bulk of Scotland's people was low, both in .
diet and possession of material goods (Weatherill, 198c
England equilibrium was achieved at an even lower level relativ
available resources which allowed a high and growing standard .
living (Wrigley and Schofield, 1981, *459–61*). In Ireland the
resources for marriage were easily available but social and political
factors kept wealth polarised and the average standard of living
low. While emphasising the broad sweep, we must be aware that
there may be important regional variations and that further
research on Scotland and Ireland is badly needed.

Conclusion

Pre-industrial societies are often lumped together as undifferentiated entities. The demographic histories of regions of the British Isles illustrates above all the great complexity and diversity of those societies. Much weight is often placed on England's distinctiveness. In certain respects this may be correct. The way population and resources were actively kept in balance by changes in nuptiality and fertility may well be unique in Europe, as may England's relatively benign mortality regime. However, other parts of the British Isles have a claim to distinctiveness. Ireland's population in the seventeenth and early eighteenth centuries was characterised by higher fertility than England's or Scotland's mainly because of an earlier age at first marriage for women but also different practices thereafter which produced higher marital fertility than in England. Child mortality may also have been higher in Ireland than in England, infant mortality higher in Scotland than in other parts of Britain and Ireland. Given that fertility was already high in Ireland, improvements in mortality may well account for the rapid population growth from the mid eighteenth century. Before that date, the difference in mortality regimes is probably more marked between Scotland and England. Relatively late marriage between the mid seventeenth and mid eighteenth century, and the possibility that marriage age and proportions ever married changed much less than in England, strengthens the impression that Scotland's place within the spectrum of north-west Europe's demographic behaviour was significantly different from England's or Ireland's. Mortality may well have been the main dynamic force.

We have dealt only in passing with the long-term economic consequences of population structures and trends. Much has been written about the role of England's low-pressure dem. regime in creating savings and other preconditions for the trial revolution. Yet, Scotland industrialised at the same tir. England from a different demographic background and a mu lower standard of living. This should warn against treating demo graphy as a determinant of economic change without considering other factors such as distribution of wealth or cultural decisions about the relative values of 'goods' such as standard of living compared with marriage and a family.

Other fields are open for research. Since the publication of *The Population History of England* in 1981, most work on that country has sought to refine the basic picture presented by Wrigley and Schofield or to relate their findings to the broader context of English society. Future work is likely to follow the same path. The possibility of regional variations in demographic patterns, the reasons behind changes in mortality and the precise relationship of nuptiality to economic opportunity are all likely to attract attention. Deeper investigation of customs surrounding infant feeding and child care may eventually explain important aspects of fertility and mortality variations. The publication of Wrigley and Schofield's volume presenting the results of family reconstitutions may well close one important chapter in English historical demography and open another.

In the rest of Britain and Ireland historians have barely begun to scratch the surface. If English historical demographers have written with one eye on the industrial revolution they must surely bend the other to the varied economic, social and demographic experiences of adjacent regions. Readers may find the tentative generalisations about population, economy and society, not to mention the lack of definite demographic statistics, on Ireland, Scotland and Wales, frustrating. Yet, these are now the true frontier lands of British historical demography. If the population history of England drew in the pioneers of the 1960s and 1970s that of the rest of Britain must attract those of the future.

Bibliography

Alldridge, N. (1986) 'The population profile of an early modern town: Chester, 1547–1728', *Annales de Démographie Historique*.

Anderson, M. (1988) *Population change in north-western Europe, 1750–1850* (London).

Appleby, A. B. (1975) 'Nutrition and disease: the case of London, 1550–1750', *Journal of Interdisciplinary History* 6.

Appleby, A. B. (1978) *Famine in Tudor and Stuart England* (Liverpool).

Bongaarts, J. (1975) 'Why high birth rates are so low', *Population and Development Review* 1.

Boulton, J. P. (1987) *Neighbourhood and society. A London suburb in the seventeenth century* (Cambridge).

Canny, N. (1985) 'Migration and opportunity: Britain, Ireland and the New World', *Irish Economic and Social History* 12.

Clark, P. (1979) 'Migration in England during the late seventeenth and early eighteenth centuries', *Past & Present* 83 or in Clark and Souden (1987).

Clark, P. and Souden, D. C. (eds) (1987) *Migration and society in early modern England* (London).

Clarkson, L. A. (1981) 'Irish population revisited, 1687–1821', in Goldstrom and Clarkson.

Clarkson, L. A. (1988) 'Conclusion: famine and Irish history', in Crawford.

Connolly, S. J. (1979) 'Illegitimacy and pre-nuptial pregnancy in Ireland before 1864: the evidence of some Catholic parish registers', *Irish Economic and Social History* 6.

Crawford E. M. (ed.) (1988) *Famine: the Irish experience, 900–1900* (Edinburgh).

Cressy, D. (1987) *Coming over. Migration and communication between England and New England in the seventeenth century* (Cambridge).

Cullen, L. M. (1975) 'Population trends in seventeenth-century Ireland', *Economic and Social Review* 6.

Cullen, L. M. (1981) 'Population growth and diet, 1600–185, strom and Clarkson.

Daultrey, S., Dickson, D. and Ó Gráda, C. (1981) 'Eighteenth Irish population: new perspectives from old sources', *Jour Economic History* 41.

De Vries, J. (1985) 'The population and economy of the preindustr. Netherlands', *Journal of Interdisciplinary History* 15.

Dickson, D. (1988) 'The gap in famines: a useful myth?', in Crawford.

Dickson, D. (1990) 'No Scythians here: women and marriage in seventeenth-century Ireland', in MacCurtain, M., and O'Dowd, M. (eds), *Women and society in early modern Ireland* (Edinburgh).

Dickson, D., Ó Gráda, C. and Daultrey, S. (1982) 'Hearth tax, household size, and Irish population growth, 1680–1800', *Proceedings of the Royal Irish Academy* 82.

Dobson, M. J. (1989a) 'Mortality gradients and disease exchanges: comparisons between old England and colonial America', *Social History of Medicine* 2.

Dobson, M. J. (1989b) 'The last hiccup of the old demographic regime', *Continuity and Change* 4.

Ekirch, A. R. (1987) *Bound for America. The transportation of British convicts to the colonies, 1718–1775.*

Eversley, D. E. C. (1981) 'The demography of the Irish Quakers, 1650–1850', in Goldstrom and Clarkson.

Finlay, R. A. P. (1978) 'The accuracy of the London parish registers, 1580–1653', *Population Studies* 32.

Finlay, R. A. P. (1981a) *Population and metropolis: the demography of London, 1580–1650* (Cambridge).

Finlay, R. A. P. (1981b) 'Differential child mortality in pre-industrial England', *Annales de Démographie Historique*.

Flinn, M. W. (ed.) (1977) *Scottish population history from the 17th century to the 1930s* (Cambridge).

Flinn, M. W. (1982) 'The population history of England, 1541–1871', *Economic History Review* 35.

Galenson, D. (1981) *White servitude in colonial America* (Cambridge).

Galloway, P. R. (1985) 'Annual variations in death by age, deaths by cause, prices, and weather in London, 1640 to 1830', *Population Studies* 39.

Gibson, A. and Smout, T. C. (1992) *Prices, food and wages in Scotland, c1550–1780* (Cambridge).

Gillespie, R. (1988) 'Meal and money: the harvest crisis of 1621–4 and the Irish economy', in Crawford.

Goldstone, J. A. (1986) 'The demographic revolution in England: a re-examination', *Population Studies* 49.

Goldstrom, J. A. and Clarkson, L. A. (eds) (1981) *Irish population, economy, and society* (Oxford).

A. P. (1984) 'Gold from dross? Population reconstruction for pre-census era', *Historical Methods* 17.

J. (1983) 'Two kinds of pre-industrial household formation system', in Wall, R. (ed.), *Family forms in historic Europe* (Cambridge).

enry, L. and Blanchet, D. (1983) 'La population de l'Angleterre de 1541 à 1871', *Population* 38.

Hollingsworth, T. H. (1964) 'The demography of the British peerage', *Population Studies* supplement to volume 18, no. 2.

Houlbrooke, R. A. (1984) *The English family, 1450–1750* (London).

Houston, R. A. (1979) 'Parish listings and social structure: Penninghame and Whithorn (Wigtownshire) in perspective', *Local Population Studies* 23.

Houston, R. A. (1985) 'Geographical mobility in Scotland, 1652–1811: the evidence of testimonials', *Journal of Historical Geography*, 11.

Houston, R. A. (1988) 'The demographic regime, 1760–1830', in Devine, T. M. and Mitchison, R. (eds), *A Social History of Modern Scotland*, volume 1.

Houston, R. A. (1990) 'Age at marriage of Scottish women, c.1660–1770', *Local Population Studies* 43.

Houston, R. A. (1991) 'Mortality in early modern Scotland: the life expectancy of advocates', *Continuity and Change* 5.

Houston, R. A. and Snell, K. D. M. (1984) 'Proto-industrialization? Cottage industry, social change and industrial revolution', *Historical Journal* 27.

Houston, R. A. and Whyte, I. D. (eds) (1989) *Scottish society, 1500–1800* (Cambridge).

Houston, R. A. and Withers, C. W. J. (1990) 'Migration and the turnover of population in Scotland, 1600–1900', *Annales de Démographie Historique.*

Husbands, C. (1987) 'Regional change in a pre-industrial society: wealth and population in England in the sixteenth and seventeenth centuries', *Journal of Historical Geography* 13.

Jones, R. E. (1980) 'Further evidence on the decline in infant mortality in pre-industrial England: north Shropshire, 1561–1810', *Population Studies* 34.

Kussmaul, A. (1981) *Servants in husbandry in early modern England* (Cambridge).

Kussmaul, A. (1990) *A general view of the rural economy of England, 1538–1840* (Cambridge).

Landers, J. (1990) 'Age patterns of mortality in London during the "long eighteenth century": a test of the "high potential" model of metropolitan mortality', *Social History of Medicine* 3.

Laslett, P. (1988) 'La parenté en chiffres', *Annales ESC* 43.

Laslett, P., Oosterveen, K. and Smith, R. (eds) (1980) *Bastar* *comparative history* (London).

Levine, D. (1977) *Family formation in an age of nascent cap* (London).

MaCafee, W. (1987) 'Pre-famine population in Ulster: evidence from t parish register of Killyman', in O'Flanagan, P. Ferguson, P. anc Whelan, K. (eds), *Rural Ireland, 1600–1900: modernisation and change* (Cork).

Macafee, W. and Morgan, V. (1981) 'Population in Ulster, 1660–1760', in Roebuck, P. (ed.), *Plantation to partition* (Belfast).

Mitchison, R. (1989) 'Webster revisited: a re-examination of the 1755 "census" of Scotland', in Devine, T. M. (ed.), *Improvement and enlightenment* (Edinburgh).

Mitchison, R. and Leneman, L. (1989) *Sexuality and social control. Scotland, 1660–1780* (Oxford).

Mokyr, J. and Ó Gráda, C. (1984) 'New developments in Irish population history, 1700–1850', *Economic History Review* 37.

Morgan, V. (1976) 'A case study of population change over two centuries: Blaris, Lisburn 1661–1848', *Irish Economic and Social History* 3.

Ó Gráda, C. (1979) 'The population of Ireland, 1700–1900: a survey', *Annales de Démographie Historique*.

Oeppen, J. (1991) 'Back-projection and inverse-projection: members of a wider class of constrained projection models', *Population Studies* 45.

Outhwaite, R. B. (ed.) (1981) *Marriage and society* (Cambridge).

Porter, R. (1987) *Disease, medicine and society in England, 1550–1860* (London).

Post, J. D. (1985) *Food shortage, climatic variability, and epidemic disease in pre-industrial Europe. The mortality peak in the early 1740s* (Ithaca).

Pressat, R. (1985) *The dictionary of demography* (English edition edited by C. Wilson, Oxford).

Rappaport, S. (1989) *Worlds within worlds: structures of life in sixteenth-century London*.

Riley, J. C. (1987) *The eighteenth-century campaign to avoid disease* (London).

Schofield, R. S. (1976) 'The relationship between demographic structure and environment in pre-industrial western Europe', in Conze, W. (ed.), *Sozialgeschichte der Familie in der Neuzeit Europas* (Stuttgart).

Schofield, R. S. (1977) 'An anatomy of an epidemic: Colyton, November 1645 to November 1646', in *The plague reconsidered. A new look at its origins and effects in 16th and 17th century England*. Local Population Studies supplement.

Schofield, R. S. (1983) 'The impact of scarcity and plenty on population change in England, 1541–1871', *Journal of Interdisciplinary History* or in Rotberg, R. and Rabb, T. K. (eds) (1985) *Hunger and ˌistory: the impact of changing food production and consumption patterns on society* (Cambridge).

ɔfield, R. S. (1985a) 'Through a glass darkly: *The Population History of England* as an experiment in history', *Journal of Interdisciplinary History* 15.

Schofield, R. S. (1985b) 'English marriage patterns revisited', *Journal of Family History* 10.

Schofield, R. S. (1986) 'Did the mothers really die? Three centuries of maternal mortality in "The World We Have Lost"', in Bonfield, L., Smith, R. M. and Wrightson, K. (eds), *The world we have gained: histories of population and social structure* (Cambridge).

Schofield, R. S. (1989) 'Family structure, demographic behaviour, and economic growth', in Walter and Schofield.

Schofield, R. S. and Wrigley, E. A. (1979) 'Infant and child mortality in England in the late Tudor and early Stuart period', in Webster, C. (ed.), *Health, medicine and mortality in sixteenth-century England* (Cambridge).

Schofield, R. S. and Wrigley, E. A. (1981) 'Remarriage intervals and the effect of marriage order on fertility', in Dupâquier, J. *et al.* (eds), *Marriage and remarriage in populations of the past* (London).

Sharpe, P. (1991) 'Literally spinsters: a new interpretation of local economy and demography in Colyton in the seventeenth and eighteenth centuries', *Economic History Review* 44.

Slack, P. (1985) *The impact of plague in Tudor and Stuart England* (London).

Smith, R. M. (1978) 'Population and its geography in England, 1500–1730', in Dodghson, R. A. and Butlin, R. A. (eds), *An historical geography of England and Wales* (London).

Smith, R. M. (1981) 'Fertility, economy and household formation in England over three centuries', *Population and Development Review* 7.

Smith, R. M. (1984) 'Some issues concerning families and their property in rural England, 1520–1800', in Smith, R. M. (ed.), *Land, kinship and life cycle* (Cambridge).

Smout, T. C. (1981) 'Scottish marriage, regular and irregular, 1500–1940', in Outhwaite.

Snell, K. D. M. (1985) *Annals of the labouring poor. Social change and agrarian England, 1600–1900.*

Souden, D. (1985) 'Demographic crisis and Europe in the 1590s', in Clark, P. (ed.), *The European crisis of the 1590s* (London).

Souden, D. (1987) ' "East, west – home's best?" Regional patterns in migration in early modern England', in Clark and Souden.

Trussell, J. (1983) 'Population under low pressure: reviews of tion history of *England*', *Journal of Economic History* 43.

Tyson, R. E. (1985) 'The population of Aberdeenshire, 1695–175̱ approach', *Northern Scotland* 6.

Tyson, R. E. (1986) 'Famine in Aberdeenshire, 1695–99: anatomy crisis', in Stevenson, D. (ed.), *From lairds to louns* (Aberdeen).

Tyson, R. E. (1988) 'Household size and structure in a Scottish burgh: Old Aberdeen', *Local Population Studies* 40.

Tyson, R. E. (1992) 'Contrasting regimes: population growth in Ireland and Scotland during the eighteenth century', in Houston, R. A., *et al.* (eds), *Conflict and identity in the social and economic history of Ireland and Scotland* (Edinburgh).

Wall, R. (1981) 'Inferring differential neglect of females from mortality data', *Annales de Démographie Historique*.

Walter, J. (1989) 'The social economy of dearth in early modern England', in Walter and Schofield.

Walter, J. and Schofield, R. (eds) (1989) *Famine, disease and the social order in early modern society* (Cambridge).

Wareing, J. (1980) 'Changes in the geographical distribution of the recruitment of apprentices to the London companies, 1486–1750', *Journal of Historical Geography* 6.

Weatherill, L. (1988) *Consumer behaviour and material culture in Britain, 1660–1760* (London).

Weir, D. (1984) 'Rather never than late: celibacy and age at marriage in English cohort fertility, 1541–1871', *Journal of Family History* 9.

Whyte, I. D. (1979) *Agriculture and society in seventeenth century Scotland* (Edinburgh).

Whyte, I. D. (1989a) 'Urbanization in early-modern Scotland: a preliminary analysis', *Scottish Economic and Social History* 9.

Whyte, I. D. (1989b) 'Population mobility in early modern Scotland', in Houston and Whyte.

Whyte, I. D. and Whyte, K. A. (1988) 'The geographical mobility of women in early modern Scotland' in Leneman, L. (ed.), *Perspectives in Scottish social history* (Aberdeen).

Willigan, J. D. and Lynch, K. A. (1982) *Sources and methods of historical demography* (London).

Wilson, C. (1984) 'Natural fertility in pre-industrial England, 1600–1799', *Population Studies* 38.

Wrightson, K. (1982) *English society, 1580–1680* (London).

Wrightson, K. and Levine, D. (1989) 'Death in Whickham', in Walter and Schofield

Wrigley, E. A. (ed.) (1966) *An introduction to English historical demography* (London).

,raphy

A. (1981) 'Marriage, fertility and population growth in eight-_th-century England', in Outhwaite.

, E. A. (1985) 'Urban growth and agriculture change: England and the continent in the early modern period', *Journal of Interdisciplinary History* 15.

rigley, E. A. (1989) 'Some reflections on corn yields and prices in pre-industrial economies', in Walter and Schofield.

Wrigley, E. A. and Schofield, R. S. (1981) *The population history of England, 1541–1871: a reconstruction* (London). Revised paperback edition 1989.

Wrigley, E. A. and Schofield, R. S. (1983) 'English population history from family reconstitution: summary results, 1600–1799', *Population Studies* 37.

Index

New Studies in Economic and Social History

Previously published as

Studies in Economic History

Titles in the series available from the Macmillan Press Limited

Economic History Society

The Economic History Society, which numbers around 3,000 members, publishes the *Economic History Review* four times a year (free to members) and holds an annual conference.

Enquiries about membership should be addressed to

The Assistant Secretary
Economic History Society
PO Box 70
Kingswood
Bristol
BS15 5TB

Full-time students may join at special rates.